FINAL DRAFT 4

Teacher's Manual

Series Editor: **Jeanne Lambert**
The New School

Wendy Asplin
University of Washington
Monica F. Jacobe
The College of New Jersey
Alan S. Kennedy
Columbia University

with
Lindsay Hansen, University of Arizona
and
Jane Stanley McGrath

CAMBRIDGE
UNIVERSITY PRESS

CAMBRIDGE
UNIVERSITY PRESS

32 Avenue of the Americas, New York NY 10013–2473, USA

Cambridge University Press is part of the University of Cambridge.

It furthers the University's mission by disseminating knowledge in the pursuit of education, learning and research at the highest international levels of excellence.

www.cambridge.org
Information on this title: www.cambridge.org/9781107495593

© Cambridge University Press 2016

First published 2016

Printed in Mexico by Editorial Impresora Apolo, S.A. de C.V.

A catalog record for this publication is available from the British Library.

ISBN 978-1-107-49557-9 Student's Book Level 4
ISBN 978-1-107-49558-6 Student's Book with Writing Skills Interactive Level 4
ISBN 978-1-107-49559-3 Teacher's Manual Level 4

Additional resources for this publication at www.cambridge.org/finaldraft

Cambridge University Press has no responsibility for the persistence or accuracy of URLs for external or third-party Internet Web sites referred to in this publication and does not guarantee that any content on such Web sites is, or will remain, accurate or appropriate. Information regarding prices, travel timetables, and other factual information given in this work is correct at the time of first printing but Cambridge University Press does not guarantee the accuracy of such information thereafter.

Art direction, book design, and photo research: emc design limited
Layout services: emc design limited

CONTENTS

INTRODUCTION **4**

STUDENT'S BOOK ANSWER KEY **12**

Unit 1 Academic Essays **12**
Psychology: Consumer Behavior

Unit 2 Narrative Essays **15**
History: Immigration

Unit 3 Cause and Effect Essays **18**
Sociology: Effects of Geographic Mobility

Unit 4 Comparison and Contrast Essays **22**
Anthropology: Food and Culture

Unit 5 Problem-Solution Essays **25**
Public Health: Media

Unit 6 Summary-Response Essays **28**
Communications: The Information Age

Unit 7 Argumentative Essays **31**
Sociology: Social Interaction

Unit 8 Test Taking **35**
Timed Writing

UNIT QUIZZES **37**

UNIT QUIZZES ANSWER KEY **68**

UNIT QUIZZES WRITING RUBRIC **72**

INTRODUCTION

Final Draft *is a four-level academic writing series for high beginning / low intermediate- to high advanced-level students of North American English.* The series prepares students to write in a college or university setting by focusing on the topics, rhetorical modes, skills, vocabulary, and grammar necessary for students to develop their academic writing. Students are given the tools to master academic writing. First, they learn and practice foundational academic writing skills essential to writing paragraphs and essays. Then, following a process-based approach, students move through the writing process, from brainstorming with graphic organizers to organizing and developing their ideas with outlines, before completing the final draft of their unit assignment.

Final Draft *provides frequent and realistic writing models.* Each unit features writing models that reinforce the concept that writing is purposeful. The Writing in the Real World article engages students and introduces them to the topic, ideas, language, and elements of structure or rhetorical mode taught in the unit. The Student Model then demonstrates the conventions of the target structure and mode. This progression from authentic text to traditional academic writing helps students new to academic discourse first understand the purpose of communicating with a given mode before turning their attention to mastering the form.

Final Draft *focuses on key academic vocabulary.* Students need to encounter high-frequency academic vocabulary and learn how to use it naturally in preparation for college-level writing. The academic phrases and collocations in the series were selected based on the findings of research into the *Cambridge English Corpus.* Analysis of this multibillion-word collection of real-life English indicates the language that is most relevant for academic writing, with a focus here on longer lexical chunks. The academic vocabulary in the series is also corpus-informed, the majority of words coming from Averil Coxhead's Academic Word List (AWL) and the remaining items taken from Michael West's General Service List (GSL). AWL words are identified as such in the index of the Student's Book.

Vocabulary items are contextualized and recycled throughout the unit. Academic collocations or academic phrases are introduced and practiced in alternating units. The writing models recycle these words and phrases in academic contexts, and in the final section of each unit students are prompted to find places where they can use these vocabulary items naturally when writing their end-of-unit assignment.

The grammar presented in **Final Draft** *is corpus-informed.* Corpus research tells us the most common grammar mistakes for specific grammar points in academic writing. Students study the most common grammar mistakes drawn from the *Cambridge Learner Corpus*, a unique collection of over 50 million examples of nonnative speakers' writing. Students then work to repair them in editing activities. At the end of the unit, students are reminded to correct these mistakes as they write their assignment, which helps promote accuracy in their writing.

Final Draft *teaches students to understand and avoid plagiarism.* The series provides a robust presentation of techniques for understanding and avoiding plagiarism. Each unit (except Unit 8) includes an overview of a common plagiarism-related issue, along with a skill-building activity. This innovative approach is pedagogical, not punitive. Many ESL students struggle with a range of issues related to plagiarism. By including realistic examples and practical activities in each unit, *Final Draft* helps students avoid plagiarism and improve their academic writing.

Writing Skills Interactive *provides extra practice in key writing skills.* This online course, which can be purchased with *Final Draft*, provides graduated instruction and practice in key writing skills to help students build confidence and fluency. Each unit provides an animated presentation of the target writing skill, along with automatically graded practice activities. Each unit closes with a quiz so students can assess their progress.

Special Sections

YOUR TURN ACTIVITIES

Each unit includes a wide variety of regular writing practice activities, including Your Turn activities which ask students to go beyond traditional practice to apply the skills, ideas, and language they have learned to their selected writing prompt. As a result, by the time they write their end-of-unit assignment, they are thoroughly prepared for the writing process because they have already practiced relevant skills and generated useful ideas and language to incorporate into their work. This makes the writing process less daunting than it would otherwise be.

DO RESEARCH ACTIVITIES

In Section 5 of *Final Draft 4* Units 1–7, students are given the opportunity to explore research topics before they write their first drafts. Presentations cover common research issues, from evaluating online sources to taking clear notes in order to avoid citation mistakes. Students then work on an activity that helps them apply what they just learned to their own essays.

Series Levels

Level	Description	CEFR Levels
Final Draft 1	Low Intermediate	A2
Final Draft 2	Intermediate	B1
Final Draft 3	High Intermediate	B2
Final Draft 4	Advanced	C1

Additional teacher resources for each level are available online at cambridge.org/finaldraft.

Final Draft 4

This book is designed for a semester-long writing course. There is enough material in the Student's Book for a course of 50 to 70 class hours. The number of class hours will vary, depending on how much of a unit is assigned outside of class and how much time a teacher decides to spend on specific elements in class. Because units are carefully designed to build toward the final writing activity, teachers are encouraged to work through each unit in chronological order. However, units can generally stand alone, so teachers can teach them in the order that best suits their needs. Unit 1 reviews the essay structure. Units 2–7 are organized by the rhetorical modes most commonly taught in an advanced writing class. Unit 8 is uniquely designed to help students prepare for timed writing assignments, including standardized writing exams.

Unit Overview and Teaching Suggestions

UNIT OPENER

Purpose
- To introduce the unit topic and academic discipline in an engaging way
- To elicit preliminary thinking about the unit theme and structure or rhetorical mode

Teaching Suggestion
Have students respond to the quote in writing by freewriting their ideas or by agreeing or disagreeing with the central message of the quote.

1 PREPARE YOUR IDEAS

In Section 1, students begin to explore the unit structure or rhetorical mode and choose their writing prompt for the unit.

Ⓐ Connect to Academic Writing

Purpose
- To introduce the unit structure or rhetorical mode in an accessible way
- To connect academic writing to students' lives and experience

Teaching Suggestion
To deepen the conversation, elicit additional examples from students of how the rhetorical mode connects to thinking they already do in their lives.

Ⓑ Reflect on the Topic

Purpose
- To show a writing prompt that elicits the rhetorical mode
- To introduce an appropriate graphic organizer for brainstorming and organizing ideas for the mode
- To choose a prompt for the unit writing assignment and begin generating ideas for the topic
- To engage students with the writing process early in the unit

Teaching Suggestion

Group students together who chose the same writing prompt and have them brainstorm ideas for the topic. Groups can then share their ideas with the class and receive immediate feedback.

2 EXPAND YOUR KNOWLEDGE

In Section 2, students learn academic vocabulary and read a real-world text that contains elements of the unit structure or rhetorical mode.

Ⓐ Academic Vocabulary

Purpose

- To introduce high-frequency academic words from the Academic Word List and the General Service List
- To focus on the meaning of the target vocabulary within a thematic context

Teaching Suggestion

Have students choose vocabulary words from the activity that they still have trouble understanding or contextualizing and write sentences using them. They can share their sentences in groups or with the class and receive immediate feedback.

Ⓑ Academic Collocations / Academic Phrases

Purpose

- To teach academic collocations and phrases that frequently occur in academic reading and writing
- To encourage the use of language chunks that will make student writing more natural and academic
- To tie academic vocabulary to the unit theme

Teaching Suggestion

Have students use the Internet to find more authentic examples of the collocations in sentences as a homework assignment. Students can then share their examples with the class or in groups.

Ⓒ Writing in the Real World

Purpose

- To provide authentic content, ideas, and language in a context related to the unit theme
- To introduce elements of the unit rhetorical mode in an authentic reading
- To recycle new academic vocabulary and collocations or phrases
- To introduce features of the unit structure or mode

Teaching Suggestion

After students have read and understood the text, assign a paragraph or section to small groups, and have students work together to explain the purpose of each sentence in the section. Sample student responses: *The first sentence <u>introduces</u> the topic, the second and third sentences <u>give background information</u> on the topic*, etc.

3 STUDY ACADEMIC WRITING

In Section 3, students read and analyze a student model of a traditional academic essay. A detailed examination of elements of the unit structure or rhetorical mode follows.

Ⓐ Student Model

Purpose

- To provide an aspirational student model for the unit structure or rhetorical mode
- To deepen understanding of writing technique through real-time analysis
- To provide a context for writing skills that will be studied in Section 4
- To familiarize students with writing prompts that can be answered using the unit mode
- To recycle academic vocabulary and collocations or phrases
- To evaluate and generate more ideas on the unit theme
- To demonstrate the organization and development of ideas in traditional academic writing

Teaching Suggestion

In small groups, have students discuss their answers to the Analyze Writing Skills tasks. Then have each group present to the class on something they noticed that they found interesting or still have questions about. This offers an opportunity to deepen the discussion on writing technique.

Ⓑ Unit Structure or Rhetorical Mode

Purpose

- To deepen understanding of the unit structure or rhetorical mode
- To explain key elements of the unit structure or rhetorical mode
- To have students practice writing elements of a paragraph or essay

Teaching Suggestion

Following the activities in this section in chronological order will ensure that students have covered all the key features of the unit structure or rhetorical mode. However, if students need less work in some areas, you may want to skip those parts in class and assign the activities for homework.

In general, practice activities, including Your Turn activities, can be completed in class and immediate feedback can be given by peers or the instructor. Alternately, these sections can be assigned as homework and brought to class for review.

4 SHARPEN YOUR SKILLS

In Section 4, students review and practice key writing skills, specific applications of grammar for writing, and ways to avoid plagiarism.

Ⓐ Writing Skill

Purpose

- To provide practice with discrete writing skills that students can apply to their unit writing assignments
- To deepen knowledge of rhetorical strategies

Teaching Suggestion

Collect writing samples from one or more of the Your Turn activities in this section. Reproduce several for the class – on the board, as handouts, on a screen – to use as an editing activity.

Ⓑ Grammar for Writing

Purpose

- To present specific applications of grammar for academic writing
- To draw attention to the most common grammar mistakes made by students
- To promote grammatical accuracy in academic writing
- To improve students' editorial skills

Teaching Suggestion

After students complete the editing task at the end of the section, have students identify elements of the unit mode (e.g., language, structure) and parts of an academic paragraph (e.g., topic sentence, examples, other supporting details).

Ⓒ Avoiding Plagiarism

Purpose

- To increase awareness of the issues surrounding plagiarism
- To build skills and strategies for avoiding plagiarism
- To provide regular practice of writing skills useful for avoiding plagiarism

Teaching Suggestion

Have one student read the student question in the Q & A aloud; all other students should listen with their books closed. Elicit possible responses from the class and then compare them to the professor's answer in the book.

5 WRITE YOUR PARAGRAPH OR ESSAY

In Section 5, students go through the steps of the writing process to a final draft of their unit writing assignment.

STEP 1: BRAINSTORM

Purpose

• To brainstorm, evaluate, and organize ideas for the student paragraph or essay

Teaching Suggestion

After students brainstorm their own ideas on paper, survey the class and list the top three to five ideas for each writing prompt on the board. Then have the students explain, evaluate, and rank the ideas.

STEP 2: DO RESEARCH

Purpose

• To build basic research skills

Teaching Suggestion

If applicable, go back to the Student Model in Section 3. Have students review the research in the Student Model and relate the Do Research presentation and practice to it.

STEP 3: MAKE AN OUTLINE

Purpose

• To help students organize their paragraphs or essays before writing

Teaching Suggestion

After students complete their outlines, have them work in pairs to explain how key ideas in their outlines connect to the overall topic or thesis of their paper. This process helps confirm that their ideas are directly relevant to the topic and allows students to consider their ideas more fully.

STEP 4: WRITE YOUR FIRST DRAFT

Purpose

• To give students the opportunity to use the language, skills, and ideas from the unit to answer their writing prompt

Teaching Suggestion

After students write their first drafts, have students work in pairs to give each other feedback before turning in their writing to you. Ask partners to underline sections they think are well-written and circle any words, sentences, or phrases that are unclear. Students can then revise for clarity before submitting their first drafts.

STEP 5: WRITE YOUR FINAL DRAFT

Purpose

- To evaluate and implement instructor/peer feedback
- To improve self-editing skills
- To write a final draft

Teaching Suggestion

Have students mark – highlight, underline, circle, number, etc. – sentences or parts of their writing that they revised based on peer or instructor feedback. This ensures students will incorporate some corrective feedback.

Assessment Program

The final section of the Teacher's Manual consists of an assessment program for *Final Draft*. It includes the following for each unit:

- Vocabulary quiz
- Grammar quiz
- Avoiding Plagiarism quiz
- Bank of additional writing prompts

Quizzes may be used individually or in combination with one or more of the others, depending on teacher and student needs. They are photocopiable, with downloadable versions available at cambridge.org/finaldraft. The Assessment Answer Key includes:

- General rubrics for academic writing (paragraphs / essays)
- Unit answer keys for vocabulary, grammar, and avoiding plagiarism quizzes

2.3 page 19

1 ACADEMIC ESSAYS

PSYCHOLOGY: CONSUMER BEHAVIOR

page 13

Possible answers:

1   He was probably referring to consumable things that we buy and sell, for example, clothes, furniture, electronic devices.
2   *Answers will vary.*
3   *Answers will vary.*

1 PREPARE YOUR IDEAS

B Reflect on the Topic page 14

 1.1 page 14

Answers will vary.

2 EXPAND YOUR KNOWLEDGE

A Academic Vocabulary page 16

 2.1 page 16

1 b	3 b	5 a	7 a
2 a	4 a	6 b	8 a

B Academic Collocations page 17

 2.2 page 17

1 c   2 d   3 a   4 b   5 e

C Writing in the Real World page 18
Possible answers:
Consuming responsibly means buying only the things you need and not wasting things. It also means buying things that are good for the environment from companies that treat their workers fairly.

If people bought fewer things, the environment might improve but there could be negative effects on the economy.

 2.3 page 19

Possible answers:

1   Buy Nothing Day is trying to change the culture of consumerism and reduce excessive consumption.
2   People have proposed changes that would make Buy Nothing Day more appealing to average shoppers and more effective. The changes include changing the perception that activists don't want people to buy anything, encouraging shoppers not to buy something rather than preventing all purchases, and encouraging shoppers not to buy anything for the entire holiday season.
3   *Answers will vary.*

2.4 page 19

Possible answers:

1   These three sentences draw the reader in: "They take out their credit cards and cut them up. They wander through department stores in single file, often walking and acting like zombies. They push empty shopping carts and buy nothing." These sentences give details about what people do on Buy Nothing Day and help readers imagine it more vividly.
2   Paragraph 3: One of the event's organizers wants to change the event so it only exposes shoppers to an alternative way of thinking about shopping.

    Paragraph 4: Another activist used to prevent people from buying anything, but now only encourages people to think about buying nothing.

    Paragraph 5: Other activists think Buy Nothing Day should encourage people not to buy anything for the entire holiday season, not just for one day.

3 STUDY ACADEMIC WRITING

A Student Model page 20

1   *advantages, disadvantages, shopping online*
2   *Possible answers:* Advantages: faster and cheaper; Disadvantages: can't touch the products; your credit card information could be stolen

Analyze Writing Skills pages 20–22

1   "As of 2012, Americans were spending over $1 trillion online. Economists predict that e-commerce will increase another 62 percent by 2016 and continue growing after that."

2 a) advantages

   b) convenient, wider range of products, saves money

3 "Online shopping is clearly more convenient than in-store shopping." Yes, it matches one point in 2b: convenient.

4 "key advantage" (para 2); "another advantage" (para 3)

5 a) better product availability

   b) Three supporting ideas: 1) online retailers have more items in stock, 2) "shoppers can buy items from anywhere in the world," 3) customers can know what is in stock at all times.

6 Yes.

7 a) "Online shopping was once an alternative approach to the retail experience, but today it is the most convenient, cost-effective way to shop for a large variety of products."

   b) "With these advantages, it seems very likely that economists' predictions about online shopping are correct: online shopping will undoubtedly become even more convenient and popular in the future."

 3.1 page 22

1 Online shopping is convenient, has a wider range of products, and saves money.

2 *Answers will vary.*

3 *Answers will vary.*

 3.2 pages 22–23

I Introduction

  Thesis statement: Online shopping is superior to shopping in stores because it's convenient, it offers consumers a wider range of products, and it saves money.

II Body Paragraph 1: Convenience

  A Takes less time to shop

  B Takes less time to receive goods

  C Good for people with limited mobility

III Body Paragraph 2: Product availability

  A More variety and items in stock

  B Can buy things not available locally

  C Consumers know what's in stock

IV Body Paragraph 3: Cost reduction

  A Fewer unplanned purchases

  B Large stock = lower prices

  C Saves money on transportation

V Conclusion

 B Academic Essays: Essay Structure

 3.3 page 24

1 c   2 b   3 a

 3.4 page 26

1 a   2 b

 3.5 page 26

1 The topic is online shopping.

2 The writer wants to communicate that shopping online has more advantages than disadvantages.

3 Yes, it includes the three points the writer will discuss in the body paragraphs: convenience, product availability, and cost reduction.

 3.6 pages 26–27

Possible answers:

Hook: A major clothing chain in the United States recently announced an amazing sale: jeans for $5.

Thesis statement: Consumers should not buy inexpensive clothing made in developing countries because it is often poor quality, the workers who make it are not always treated well, and it takes jobs away from our own country.

3.7 page 27

Possible answer:

In the past, products were made to last. When you bought a refrigerator or a car, you could expect to enjoy it for decades. Now, however, many of the things we buy, especially electronic devices like computers and cell phones, are useless after only a year or two. This is called *planned obsolescence*. Companies design products that they know will have to be replaced after a short period of time.

1 Online shopping is more convenient than in-store shopping.

2 *more convenient*

3 "One example of this is the world's first Internet shopper, Jane Snowball, who ordered groceries to be delivered when she broke her hip."

4 "As of May 2014, Amazon.com had 108 distribution centers."

5 "The first reason why online shopping is more convenient is that it takes less time than traditional shopping."

6 "As of May 2014, Amazon.com had 108 distribution centers."

7 "easy to see"

 3.10 page 29

Possible answers:

Topic sentence: One reason that consumerism is good for the economy is that it creates new jobs.

Supporting sentence 1: When people shop more, businesses grow.

Detail sentence: This means that businesses need to hire more people to make and sell the things people buy.

Supporting sentence 2: Other types of jobs also benefit from consumerism.

Detail sentence: For example, companies that deliver purchases to consumers do very well, and hire more drivers, when people shop more.

Concluding sentence: Clearly, consumerism creates new jobs and that is obviously a good thing for the economy.

 3.12 pages 30–31

Possible answers:

Body paragraph 1

1 One of the ways retailers can attract local customers is by giving back to the community.

2 gives money to support local schools and parks

3 ask their employees to volunteer their time for local charity groups

4 can appeal to customers by helping to improve the local community

Body paragraph 2

1 Another way retailers can appeal to customers is by hiring local residents.

2 are much more likely to buy that company's products

3 will encourage their friends and family to shop at the local business where they work

4 that hiring local residents is an excellent way for companies to appeal to customers

Body paragraph 3

1 Finally, retailers can attract customers by selling products that appeal to the local market.

2 a supermarket might sell bread, candy, and other foods that are made by local businesses

3 businesses can sell specialty products that are particularly popular in their area

4 selling products that appeal to the local market is an excellent way to gain more customers

 3.13 page 31

Possible answer:

In the future, more and more companies around the world will be doing business in an ethical way.

4 SHARPEN YOUR SKILLS

Ⓐ Writing Skill: Thesis Statements

page 32

 4.1 pages 33–34

A

1 c   2 c

B

Possible answers:

1 **a**, **b**, and **d** don't answer the prompt because they don't say whether the ads should be banned. **c** is the only option that actually says whether the ads should be banned.

2 **a** and **b** don't answer the prompt, which is asking why people buy impulsively. **d** answers the prompt but does not give specific reasons, so it is not as good as **c**. **c** is the best choice because it not only answers the prompt but also gives three reasons.

 4.2 page 34

Possible answers:

1b Internet ads should not be banned because they are a good way for businesses to target new consumers, they allow popular websites to be free of charge, and many consumers appreciate them.

2d There are three things that lead to impulse buying: where products are placed in the stores, the way they are priced, and the advertising campaigns behind them.

B Grammar for Writing: Gerunds and Infinitives page 35

4.4 page 36

1 buying
2 to spend
3 teaching
4 to pay
5 telling
6 to purchase
7 going
8 buying
9 to get
10 growing up

4.5 page 37

1 being included
2 to be interviewed
3 to be evaluated
4 to be … informed
5 being exposed
6 to be seen

Avoiding Common Mistakes page 38

4.6 page 38

Email advertising from retail stores ~~give~~ *gives*
customers access to great deals, but is it effective?
Studies show that filling people's inboxes with
more and more advertising ~~force~~ *forces* them to think
about the company, but does not always convince
them to shop. Many companies think that
customers will want ~~buying~~ *to buy* things when they
receive these messages, and that is good enough
for them (Davidson 6). However, a Gallup poll
taken in 2011 showed that consumers choose
to delete these messages 65 percent of the time.
The same study showed that people fail to take
advantage of the advertised deals 61 percent
of the time. Studies also show that consumers
tend ~~removing~~ *to remove* themselves from mailing lists
after deleting advertising messages for more
than three months. As a result, some companies
are considering ~~to change~~ *changing* the way they practice
email advertising. Many of these companies are
discussing ~~to use~~ *using* text messaging and social media
as alternatives to email marketing. Clearly, email
advertising may not be working well enough for
some companies to continue using it.

C Avoiding Plagiarism page 39

4.7 page 40

1 a   2 b   3 a

4.8 page 40

Levitt, Steven. *Freakonomics.* New York: Morrow,
2006. Print.

4.9 page 40

Yarrow, Kit. "Why Clearance Sales Are
Psychologically 'Irresistable.'" *Psychology Today.*
Psychology Today, 17 Jan. 2013. Web. 30 Mar.
2014.

5 WRITE YOUR ESSAY

STEP 1: BRAINSTORM PAGE 41

1 Ideas not used: Fun!; Better for environment –
   less pollution; Healthier – better for shoppers,
   less stress

2 NARRATIVE ESSAYS

HISTORY: IMMIGRATION

page 47
Possible answers:

1 To say that you and your classmates are "in the
   same boat" means that you are in the same
   situation.
2 No matter what country they came from, all
   immigrants face the same challenges when they
   arrive in a new country.
3 For education, for better work or economic
   opportunities, to get away from problems
   in their home country, to be closer to family
   members, to have a better quality of life.

1 PREPARE YOUR IDEAS

B Reflect on the Topic page 48

1.1 page 48

1 Yes. The beginning is when the writer learns he is
   moving from Mexico and he arrives in the United
   States. The middle is when things get worse at
   school and at home. The ending is when his
   grades finally improve and he makes friends.

2 *Possible answer:* The story will be interesting, but the writer will need to tell more about how he was able to make friends and improve his grades, and what helped him change.

2 EXPAND YOUR KNOWLEDGE

A Academic Vocabulary page 50

 2.1 page 50

A
1 b   2 c   3 d   4 a
B
1 b   2 c   3 a   4 d

B Academic Phrases page 51

 2.2 page 51

1 c   2 a   3 b

C Writing in the Real World page 52
Possible answers:

Some common struggles immigrants often have include difficulties adjusting to a new language, culture, customs, and climate; problems finding work; difficulties making new friends; and missing friends and family from home.

"Silent struggle" might mean that the author is having difficulties after immigrating but isn't able to talk to anyone about them or explain his problems and feelings clearly.

 2.3 page 53

1 The writer considers the idea of returning to Ghana because he finds life in the United States stressful and full of complexities.
2 The writer expected his trip to be relaxing, but instead he is full of conflict about whether to return to Ghana permanently or stay in the United States.
3 *Answers will vary.*

 2.4 page 53

1 b   2 a

3 STUDY ACADEMIC WRITING

A Student Model page 54

1 The prompt is asking the writer to tell a story that ends with him or her changing their view of the world or learning an important lesson.
2 *Possible answers:* understanding the language, making new friends, missing friends and family from home, following the rules at a new school

Analyze Writing Skills pages 54–56

1 a
2 a
3 negative feelings: lonely, excluded, different, ashamed, worried
4 a 4
  b 3
5 No (The subjects are "I," "I," "they.")
6 a

 3.1 page 56

1 The writer gained a new perspective by realizing the sacrifices his grandparents had made for him. This change was caused by seeing his grandmother cry and talk about how much she missed Mexico, and hearing his grandfather say that they were making sacrifices for the grandchildren. The positive consequences for the writer were a new perspective, learning English fluently, and feeling more comfortable in the United States.
2 The party shows that the character is grateful to his grandparents and that he is comfortable with both the Mexican and American parts of his life.
3 *Possible answers:* missing friends and family from home, problems getting used to the local weather or food, difficulties making new friends, problems adjusting to local customs and rules

 3.2 page 56

I Introduction
Thesis Statement: <u>Lacked perspective</u>; couldn't see beyond self
II Hard time adjusting
  A Felt different
    1 Felt lonely and left out
    2 Felt different from the other students
  B Ashamed
    1 Ashamed of problems with English
    2 <u>Grandparents' greeting at school</u>; felt embarrassing

III One day came home early
- A Heard grandparents talking about missing Mexico
  - 1 Grandmother <u>looking at old pictures and crying</u>; she missed Mexico
  - 2 Grandfather mentioned <u>sacrifices for grandchildren</u>
- B Felt ashamed

IV I gained new perspective
- A Understood complexity of their lives and their sacrifice
  - 1 Grandparents never expressed anything but positive thoughts
- B Decided to work hard and make grandparents happy
  - 1 Learned English and felt more comfortable

V Conclusion
- A Grandparents' fortieth anniversary party
  - 1 Traditional Mexican food and music
  - 2 A way of repaying grandparents
- B Lesson learned: <u>new opportunities and new perspective</u> were grandparents' gifts

 Narrative Essays page 58

 3.3 page 59

1 story
2 teach
3 • thesis • details • climax

 3.4 page 60

Idea **c** would probably make the best story in response to the writing prompt. It has a clear lesson that is communicated by the story, there is a clear conflict (between the two drivers), it has interesting scenes with dialogue, and it can be told in one essay.

 3.6 page 61

B is the better introductory paragraph because it has more details that draw in the reader. For example, the writer talks about the weather, feeling a sense of hope, and details about the background to the story. Similar details could be added to improve paragraph **A**.

 3.8 pages 61–62

b is the best thesis for the introduction because it answers the prompt and is a better fit with the background information.

 3.10 page 64

1 "I do not really like ice cream."
"The restaurant was on Smith Street."
2 "large, jolly sort of woman," "finally lost her happy face," "wrapped our arms around her knees"
3 "I'm right here," she said. [Punctuation Mistake 1: Punctuation after "said" should be a period, not a comma.] "Do not worry. Your mother will return."
"I told you I would not come home until I found a job," she explained.
"Mama," we shouted. "Where were you?" [Punctuation Mistake 2: No comma after "Where were you?"]

 3.11 page 65

"She started to yell as she pulled out the letter approving our visa."

4 SHARPEN YOUR SKILLS

A Writing Skill 1: Parallel Structure
page 66

 4.1 page 66

1 got married
2 one of the youngest Supreme Court justices
3 served as editor of the *Yale Law Journal*.
4 skills, knowledge, confidence
5 political views, judicial philosophy
6 has many fans there, is often invited to speak

B Writing Skill 2: Sentence Variety
page 67

4.2 page 68

1 After the "Gold Rush" of 1849, Chinese workers began immigrating to the United States in large numbers.
2 Uncle Lee, my father's great-great-granduncle, was one of tens of thousands of Chinese immigrants who landed in San Francisco in the early 1850s and settled just north of the city.
3 Although some prospectors did find gold, it was not as easy to find as he had expected.
4 According to my father, life was hard for Uncle Lee and other Chinese immigrants. They were discriminated against and sometimes even attacked by American prospectors.

5 For example, in the town of Weaverville, north of San Francisco, Chinese settlers established a Taoist temple that is still there today.

C Grammar for Writing: Past Tense Forms page 69

 4.3 page 70

1 a   2 a   3 b   4 b   5 b   6 a

Avoiding Common Mistakes page 71

 4.4 page 71

In 1882, the U.S. Congress ~~was passing~~ *passed* a law called the Chinese Exclusion Act. This law stated that immigrant workers from China were no longer allowed to immigrate to the United States and could not be citizens. Chinese laborers had *been* coming to the United States since the "Gold Rush" more than 40 years before. Rumors of a "mountain of gold" in California started in Hong Kong in 1849, and quickly spread throughout the provinces of China. This brought thousands of Chinese immigrants to America's west coast. These immigrants added an Asian influence to a country that it ~~has~~ *had* not had previously. Still, this influence remained limited because the Chinese Exclusion Act ~~is~~ *was* in effect. In fact, this act was a form of discrimination, since the Chinese were the only ethnic or national group that was not allowed to immigrate. Although the law was supposed to only be temporary, Congress ~~was making~~ *made* it permanent in 1902. They also added new restrictions by stating that each Chinese resident had to register and obtain a certificate of residence. By this time, because so many Chinese Americans were excluded from the mainstream of American life, they ~~have~~ *had* formed "Chinatown" communities where they supported each other. However, things changed during World War II.

Many Chinese-American men had *been* fighting in the U.S. military against Japan and helping in the American war effort. The government decided that they had to change their attitude toward Chinese Americans and end the discriminatory law. In 1943, the Exclusion Act was finally ~~being~~ eliminated.

D Avoiding Plagiarism page 72

 4.5 page 73

1, 3, 5

 4.6 page 73

"Between 1870 and 1930, there were 30 million new immigrants to the U.S."
"In 2012, over 750,000 people became U.S. citizens, mostly in California, New York, and Florida."

3 CAUSE AND EFFECT ESSAYS

SOCIOLOGY: EFFECTS OF GEOGRAPHIC MOBILITY

page 79

1 Huntington meant that history is the result of "man's migrations." The sum total of the evidence of these migrations is our history.
2 *Answers will vary.*
3 *Answers will vary.*

1 PREPARE YOUR IDEAS

B Reflect on the Topic page 80

 1.1 page 80

Possible answers:
Causes for writing prompt 1: not enough houses or apartments in rural areas, gasoline too expensive to live in rural areas
Effects for writing prompt 2: more older adults learning Spanish, more Spanish signs in restaurants and public places, more interest in Latin American holidays and festivals

2 EXPAND YOUR KNOWLEDGE

Ⓐ Academic Vocabulary page 82

2.1 pages 82–83

1 a	3 b	5 b	7 a
2 b	4 a	6 a	8 a

Ⓑ Academic Collocations page 83

2.2 page 83

1 b   2 b   3 a   4 a   5 b

Ⓒ Writing in the Real World page 84

Possible answers:

Moving might be tough for kids because they have to make new friends and get used to a new school. Some things might be easier for kids than for adults who move, such as learning a new language.

2.3 page 85

1 According to the article, one of the effects of moving on children is disrupting important friendships. Also, the article says that adults who moved frequently as children do not feel as satisfied with their lives and can have relationship troubles.

2 The author's son had trouble sleeping and paying attention, and he was often sad. This evidence is not very convincing because it only shows what happened to one person and the author doesn't say whether he reacted this way for just a short period or for several years. The results of a survey of many people from different backgrounds would be better evidence.

3 *Answers will vary.*

2.4 page 85

Possible answers:

1 The first paragraph is mostly about the effects of something. Words and phrases that show us this: "are affected by," "these effects"

2 The second paragraph is mostly about the causes of something. Words and phrases that show us this: "because of"

3 STUDY ACADEMIC WRITING

Ⓐ Student Model page 86

1 The writer will focus on a cause and effect relationship involving young people moving out of rural communities.

2 The essay will be about causes. The writer will focus on things that have recently caused young people to move out of rural communities.

Analyze Writing Skills pages 86–87

1 multiple causes

2 reason, key factor

3 McGranahan, Cromartie, and Wojan; "Population"

4 a

3.1 page 87

1 People are moving away from rural areas because these places lack economic opportunities, entertainment options, and accessible health care.

2 Paragraphs 2, 3, and 4 deal with reasons people leave rural communities.

3 *Answers will vary.*

3.2 pages 88–89

I Introduction
Thesis statement: Outmigration happens for many reasons, but the most important are fewer job opportunities, lack of amenities, and inaccessible health care.

II Limited number of decent employment opportunities
A Fewer good jobs and more competition
  1 Young people want good careers (McGranahan)
  2 Accounting example
B Jobs in larger cities usually have a higher salary
  1 Paralegal example

III Rural areas often do not have a lot of conveniences
A Young people leave areas that are not attractive and exciting (McGranahan)
  1 My opinion – young people want to learn and experience new things
B When people retire, they leave for better services and conveniences

IV Lack of access to health care makes people leave
  A 90 percent of physicians work in cities (NCSL)
     1 Families with children have to travel far for health care
     2 Older adults do not get the medical attention that they need
V Conclusion

B Cause and Effect Essays: Organization page 89

 3.3 page 90

Organization A
1 F   2 F   3 T
Organization B
1 T   2 T   3 F

 3.4 page 91

Circled words in Paragraph 1:

struggling cities … steadily declining and struggling, too … a 2014 Census report showed that as of July 2013 almost two thirds of rural counties had become smaller

Thesis: "Outmigration happens for many reasons, but some common factors are fewer good job opportunities, lack of amenities, and inaccessible health care."

Words that show the focus is on causes: for many reasons … some common factors are …

 3.5 page 91

Possible answers:
1 People immigrate for many reasons, but the most important ones are for education, for economic reasons, and to escape dangerous situations in their home countries.
2 Although moving to a new home can have negative effects for some, the positive effects are much greater, including opportunities to make new friends, learn about new places, and pursue job opportunities.

 3.7 page 94

Possible answer:
One important reason people immigrate is for better job opportunities.

 3.8 page 94

Possible answer:
One stressful effect of moving is that people encounter many unexpected expenses. This is because moving belongings to a new home can often have hidden costs, such as the cost of boxes, tape, padding, gasoline, and tips for movers. If the new home is rented, the landlord may require extra money as a security deposit, so this is also an unexpected expense. People who buy a home may also have to pay more because of repairs they did not expect to have to make. For these reasons, the hidden costs of moving can be significant.

 3.9 pages 94–95

1 a   2 b   3 a   4 a   5 b

 3.11 page 96

Possible answer:
With a positive, confident mindset, parents can help their children see moving as an exciting adventure that will greatly enhance their lives.

4 SHARPEN YOUR SKILLS

A Writing Skill 1: Paraphrasing
page 97

4.1 page 98

Possible answers:
1 In "Moving Is Tough for Kids," Nancy Darling states that middle-class children are less likely to move than children in wealthy and poor families.
2 According to the Center for Rural Pennsylvania, when people move out of rural Pennsylvania, they relocate to counties where there are more new businesses and more jobs that pay more money.
3 The United Nations Population Fund states two main reasons why people move within their own countries. People migrate in search of more opportunities, resources, or services, or to get away from problems such as violent crime and natural disasters.
4 According to Stephen Bochner, there are two main ways that cultures interact: when people from one culture travel to another place, and when people interact in a society that already has many different cultures.

B Writing Skill 2: Avoiding Fragments, Run-On Sentences, and Comma Splices page 99

 4.2 page 100

Possible answers:

1 Moving from one city to another can be challenging but rewarding.
2 Tourism has helped the global economy, but it has harmed the environment.
3 Everyone who comes to the United States must have a visa. People who work in the U.S. must get a special kind of visa and must be supported by a company in a particular field.
4 It has always been challenging for immigrant job applicants to be treated equally; they are viewed as less important than citizens.
5 Many believe moving to a warm location like Florida is easy for everyone, but recent research shows that changing climates can cause depression and anxiety.

C Grammar for Writing: Present Perfect and Present Perfect Progressive page 100

 4.3 page 101

1 have experienced / have been experiencing
2 have developed
3 have increased / have been increasing
4 have been protesting
5 has been
6 have lived / have been living

Avoiding Common Mistakes page 102

 4.4 pages 102–103

Culture shock is common when moving to a new country, but many people experience cultural difficulties when moving between regions within large countries like the United States. A new study released by Progress University examines how moving to New England (a group of states in the northeastern United States) from many other parts of America comes with challenges. Dr. Rudolph
been
Abrams has ‸ studying 25 families that are new to New England for the last five years, gathering data on community and school integration and measuring mood. His completed study shows that
have
most of these 25 families ~~has~~ reported missing favorite foods not available in local grocery stores.
described
Others have ~~been describing~~ the initial difficulty they experienced years ago getting to know people in workplaces, schools, and community groups. However, those families now report significant improvement in their local relationships and increased satisfaction with the move to New England. Other data shared from the study include trouble with accented English. In one example response quoted by the researchers, a father of
been
two said that he "has ‸ working with a man whose accent [he] could not understand. Assuming the man was a new immigrant, [he] asked what country he grew up in and was embarrassed to be told America – and Maine" (Abrams et al. 6). The same man reported that he had never lived outside Alabama and never traveled outside the region until moving north for his new job (7). Dr. Abrams and his colleagues have already ~~been~~
spent
~~spending~~ more than five years studying these subjects and will expand the research to other families in the future. All said, this work so far has presented concrete evidence for something that
been
has ‸ coming up in conversations about national migration for a long time.

D Avoiding Plagiarism page 104

 4.5 page 105

1 The paraphrase is not accurate. A *householder* is a person who is in charge of their home. The person moves, not the house.
2 The paraphrase is not accurate. The quote says that 13.7% of householders who lived with their children moved. This is not the same as saying 13.7% of all children moved.
3 The paraphrase is accurate, but the writer did not cite the source.

4.6 page 105

Possible answer:

According to David Ihrke of the U.S. Census Bureau, in 2012 about 14% of parents with children at home moved.

4 COMPARISON AND CONTRAST ESSAYS

ANTHROPOLOGY: FOOD AND CULTURE

page 111

1 The quotation means that we can learn a lot about someone from the food they prefer to eat.
2 *Answers will vary.*
3 *Answers will vary.*

1 PREPARE YOUR IDEAS

B Reflect on the Topic page 112

 1.1 page 112

Possible answers:

Differences: Foods with artificial ingredients have different colors from foods with natural ingredients.

Similarities: Both are available in most supermarkets.

2 EXPAND YOUR KNOWLEDGE

A Academic Vocabulary page 114

2.1 page 114

A
| 1 c | 2 d | 3 a | 4 b |

B
| 1 b | 2 d | 3 a | 4 c |

B Academic Phrases page 115

2.2 page 115

| 1 c | 2 a | 3 b |

C Writing in the Real World page 116

Possible answer:

The "cost" the title is referring to is not the direct cost in money but the way the global food system has negative effects (or "costs") to the environment, the economy, and people's health.

 2.3 page 117

Possible answers:

1 The impact is negative because the ships take on toxic fuel and the transportation system causes pollution.
2 It has encouraged unhealthy eating habits.
3 *Answers will vary.*

 2.4 page 117

1 The first two paragraphs compare garlic from China with garlic grown locally in California.
2 *whereas*
3 *Similarly*

3 STUDY ACADEMIC WRITING

A Student Model page 118

1 The prompt is asking the writer to compare natural foods and foods with artificial ingredients.
2 *Possible answer:*
   The writer might mention differences in the way "artificial" and "natural" are defined, what they cost, and the effect on the environment.

Analyze Writing Skills pages 118–120

1 *artificial foods, natural foods*
2 "However, when comparing their definitions, prices, and impact on the environment, it soon becomes clear that artificial foods are not always the inferior choice."
   Circled topics: *definitions, prices, impact on the environment*
3 "One advantage of artificial foods is that they have a clearer definition than natural foods." The writer will discuss artificial foods first.
4 Underline: "foods with artificial ingredients benefit consumers more."
   Double underline: "They usually have lower prices"; "In contrast, natural ingredients must be grown on a farm, processed, and then transported to the lab"; "Furthermore, natural foods have become a valuable commodity in the United States."

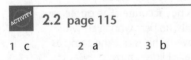

5 *In contrast*

6 "For example, it is important to note that putting real fruit in a product means that people must first develop the land to grow it. They may have to cut down other trees to make room for new crops. In addition, they must water the crops regularly to keep them alive."

7 Restate main ideas: "The 'natural' label can be used by U.S. companies to charge more for food that might not truly be healthier, whereas "artificial" has a more transparent definition. Using artificial ingredients saves consumers money and also reduces the amount of land and water needed to grow natural ingredients."
Comment by the writer: "I no longer believe that natural is always better, and I have altered my shopping habits as a result. Now when I go grocery shopping in the United States, there are many artificial foods in my cart."

 3.1 page 120

1 The two subjects are contrasted in order to show the reasons why one of them is a better choice.

2 *Answers will vary.*

3 *Answers will vary.*

 3.2 pages 120–122

I Introduction
Thesis statement: However, when comparing their definitions, prices, and impact on the environment, it soon becomes clear artificial foods are not always the inferior choice.

II Body paragraph 1: Definition
  A Artificial foods have clearer definition
    1 Restricted to one meaning
    2 Refers to foods with man-made chemicals
  B Natural foods no legal definition
    1 FDA doesn't want to define them
    2 Can refer to whatever companies want it to mean

III Body paragraph 2: Benefits to consumers
  A Artificial foods benefit consumers more
    1 Lower prices – made in a lab
  B Natural foods more expensive
    1 Expensive to grow
    2 High demand so price is higher

IV Body paragraph 3: Impact on the environment
  A Environmental advantage of artificial foods
    1 Manufacturing does not require farmland or crops

  B Natural foods more demanding of environment
    1 Requires land
    2 Must cut down trees for land
    3 Use a lot of water

V Conclusion
  A Restatement of thesis
  B Comment

B Comparison and Contrast Essays
page 122

 3.3 page 124

The writer used point-by-point organization. He probably chose this organization because the two subjects had many differences related to each point.

 3.4 page 124

1 F   2 T   3 F   4 T

 3.5 page 126

Body Paragraph 1: Point 1: drinks
Subject A: 100 years ago – tea
Detail: traditional
Detail: cheap and available
Subject B: Today – coffee
Detail: very popular
Detail: readily available
Detail: status symbol

 3.7 page 127

1 T   2 T   3 F

3.9 page 128

Possible answers:
Fast food and slow food eaters have very different enjoyments and routines. Fast food eaters enjoy being busy with work and other activities and do not have time to sit down for a long meal. Slow food eaters, on the other hand, enjoy spending a long time preparing and eating food. They also tend to have more free time in their daily routine than fast food eaters.
Another difference is how concerned they are about their health. Fast food eaters often do not spend a lot of time worrying about how the food they eat will affect their bodies. They want something cheap and filling so they

won't feel hungry. Slow food eaters are different because they are very concerned about how food affects their health, and they usually prefer to use healthier ingredients and cooking styles.

Finally, they have entirely different tastes in food. Fast food eaters usually prefer burgers, pizza, fries, and other food that has meat and fat and is fried. Slow food eaters prefer vegetables, fruit, and other foods that can be eaten fresh. They do not eat meat often and prefer their meat to be cooked in a slow, healthy way.

 3.11 page 129

In summary, artificial foods are superior to natural foods in certain ways. The "natural" label can be used by U.S. companies to charge more for food that might not truly be healthier, whereas "artificial" has a more transparent definition. Using artificial ingredients saves consumers money and also reduces the amount of land and water needed to grow natural ingredients. The differences between artificial and natural foods are much more complex than I had first assumed. I no longer believe that natural is always better, and I have altered my shopping habits as a result. Now when I go grocery shopping in the United States, there are many artificial foods in my cart.

4 SHARPEN YOUR SKILLS

A Writing Skill 1: Words and Phrases That Show Similarities and Differences page 130

 4.1 pages 130–131

2 Similar to information, food is now exchanged very easily between countries because of globalization.

3 Even though rice actually originated in Asia, it is a common ingredient in Mexican cuisine.

4 Fast food from big international chains is considered cheap in the United States. However, in Russia, it is much less affordable.

5 Indian restaurants typically do not serve beef. In contrast, Argentinian restaurants are known for their many ways of preparing beef.

6 Both haggis, a traditional Scottish dish, and drob, a Romanian dish served at Easter, are cooked in a sheep's stomach.

B Writing Skill 2: Coherence page 131

 4.3 page 132

1 Furthermore / In addition
2 In addition
3 With regard to / Regarding / With respect to
4 With regard to / Regarding / With respect to
5 First
6 Next
7 With regard to / Regarding / With respect to
8 in sum

 4.4 page 133

1 this study / this book
2 This belief
3 These
4 This
5 The / This
6 They

C Grammar for Writing: Appositives page 134

 4.5 pages 134–135

1 A division of PepsiCo, Frito-Lay sells potato chips in China.

2 An example of a popular Lebanese dish is *baba ghanuj*, a kind of eggplant salad.

3 An Italian explorer, Christopher Columbus was sent by the king and queen of Spain to see if he could reach Asia by sailing west.

4 An early example of the globalization of food was the trading of spices along the Silk Road, a group of routes that linked China with Central Asia and Europe.

5 One kind of cheese which can only be made in Italy is Parmigiano-Reggiano, a kind of hard cheese.

Avoiding Common Mistakes page 135

 4.6 page 135

Because of the United States' special history of immigration, American food has been influenced by cuisines from all over the world. A melting pot, *a* large pot used to melt multiple ingredients together over heat, has often been used as a symbol of American society and culture. It's true that some food considered "American" did not originate here. Hamburgers and hot dogs, very common American sandwiches, were brought by German immigrants. Sometimes, food brought by immigrants adapts to American life just as the immigrants do. Chop suey, a dish of mixed meat and vegetables in a thick sauce, is served at Chinese restaurants in the United States but was not eaten in China. Mayonnaise, ~~that~~ a very common American condiment, actually comes from Europe. These are just a few examples of culinary adaptation in the United States.

D Avoiding Plagiarism page 136

 4.7 page 137

Best sources: 2, 5, 6

5 PROBLEM–SOLUTION ESSAYS

PUBLIC HEALTH: MEDIA

page 143

1 Carlyle compared good health to having hope because he thinks people who have hope have the most important thing in life.
2 *Answers will vary.*
3 *Answers will vary.*

1 PREPARE YOUR IDEAS

B Reflect on the Topic page 144

 1.1 page 144

Possible answers: Write to the drug companies or hospitals and ask for a discount. Have the treatment done in another country where health care costs are lower.

A Academic Vocabulary page 146

 2.1 pages 146–147

A
1 b   2 d   3 a   4 c
B
1 b   2 d   3 c   4 a

B Academic Collocations page 147

2.2 page 147

1 d   2 a   3 e   4 b   5 c

C Writing in the Real World page 148
Possible answers:
People can solve this problem by avoiding health websites or by speaking to their doctor before checking online.

 2.3 page 149

1 The author thinks cyberchondria might be a problem because a poll showed that 61 percent of Americans use the Internet for medical information, and other studies have shown "wide levels of increased anxiety triggered by this habit."
2 Kwan's study found that people who saw the most mild, common symptoms listed together were more likely to believe they had the disease. She thinks this is because cyberchondriacs jump to the conclusion that if they have some symptoms they must have all of them. She relates this to the way gamblers think that if they win a couple of times they are on a "winning streak."
3 *Answers will vary.*

2.4 page 149

1 Problem: paragraph 1; keywords: *It's a familiar story, now increasingly common*
Solution: paragraph 5; keywords: *help decrease anxiety, They could do this by*
2 Evidence why cyberchondria is a problem: poll results and studies in paragraph 1. Keywords: *According to a 2009 Pew poll, other recent studies have shown*

3 STUDY ACADEMIC WRITING

Ⓐ Student Model page 150

1 The central problem in the prompt is the debt that some families have from medical bills.

2 Yes, the writer will have to provide background on both the problem and the solution.

3 *Answers will vary.*

Analyze Writing Skills pages 150–152

1 a

2 c

3 "Crowdfunding is a practical and effective way for Americans struggling with medical costs to get help."

4 b

5 "Crowdfunding is an excellent solution because it is easy to get started, and the results are usually good."

6 b

7 a

8 "In short, it is a shame that medical costs are unreasonably high and that seriously ill people need to ask others for help in a country as rich as ours."

3.1 page 152

1 The writer thinks the problem is important because medical bills are the number-one cause of financial problems in the United States.

2 *Answers will vary.*

3 The writer says that fund-raising events seem like a good idea but are too expensive, take too much time and effort, and only attract local donors.

3.2 pages 152–154

I Introduction
Thesis statement: Crowdfunding is a practical and effective way for Americans struggling with medical costs to get help.

II Body paragraph 1: Financial difficulty from medical bills
  A High medical costs
    1 75% of Americans can't find $2,000 in an emergency
    2 Average cancer patient pays $8,500 per year
  B Loss of wages is another problem
    1 Families can't afford their bills anymore.
    2 Over 62% of bankruptcies caused by medical expenses
  C Anxiety also a related problem

III Body paragraph 2: Crowdfunding is easy and effective.
  A Fund-raising websites
    1 Web page shared on social media
    2 Contributors can donate as much as they want
  B The Kennet family
    1 Needed financial support for cancer treatment
    2 Raised $57,000 online
    3 Received emotional support as well

IV Body paragraph 3: Fund-raising events not as effective
  A High ticket prices
    1 Fund-raising concert too expensive
  B Too much time and effort required
  C Only attract local donors

V Conclusion

Ⓑ Problem–Solution Essays page 154

3.3 page 155

1 Introduction
2 Introduction / Body paragraph 1
3 Body paragraph 1
4 Body paragraph 2
5 Body paragraph 3
6 Conclusion

3.4 page 156

Explains what the problem is: 1, 3
Describes who the problem affects and how it affects them: 1, 2, 3, 4, 5, 6
Explains why the problem still needs to be solved: 7

3.5 page 156

Possible answers:

1 "Social media" **refers to** websites that allow users to share information and connect with each other.

2 **The problem** with social media **is that** users often exaggerate or lie about their activities.

3 **A secondary problem is** that people constantly check social media sites for updated information on their friends instead of contacting them directly.

4 **While** time wasting is one effect of social media, **the most urgent issue** is the feeling of inadequacy some users have as a result of using social media.

5 Depression and anxiety **have become a serious problem because** people tend to compare the amount of input they provide on these sites with the amount provided by other people.

 3.7 page 158

Words or phrases that show the solution: *is an excellent solution because*

 3.8 page 158

Possible answers:

2 Intensive addiction counseling can be a solution because it helps people understand the reasons for their behavior.

3 The problem of Internet addiction can be solved by psychological treatment.

4 One recent study demonstrates that in-patient addiction counseling would solve the problem.

 3.10 page 160

Describe the alternative solution and why some people think it would work: 1

Give disadvantages of the alternative solution: 2, 5, 7

Give a fact, example, or statistic to show the weakness of the solution: 3

Explain why the writer's solution is better: 4, 6, 8

 3.12 page 162

The Internet has changed the world in so many positive ways. Who would have thought that an addiction to it could harm people and do real damage to their lives? The thousands of Americans who have sought counseling for Internet addiction have realized this. Their loved ones have as well because they have seen family members lose jobs, friends, and lives because they became addicted to the Internet. As online life grows more important to professional and academic lives each year, Internet addiction becomes a more important problem to solve. By treating …

 3.13 page 162

Possible answers:

1 The thesis does not give a reason why the solution would work, e.g., *It can be solved by involving parents and school officials, who have the ability to identify and punish cyberbullies.*

2 The thesis mentions all of the needed elements.

 3.15 page 163

Possible answer: Sentence 2 is better at reminding readers about the problem and solution. It gives more detail about the problem (*risk worry and anxiety for themselves and their doctors … deceptive websites will always be out there*) and the solution (*evaluate health information and its sources*).

4 SHARPEN YOUR SKILLS

Ⓐ Writing Skill 1: Introduction to Summarizing page 164

 4.1 page 164

1 • give the author's full name and explain who he or she is: A = no; B = yes
   • say where and when the text was published: A = no; B = yes
   • include the important details from the article: A = yes; B = yes
   • not include unimportant details: A = no (the details about the screenshot and the representative's response are not important); B = yes (all details included are important)

2 Summary B is better because it is more complete and does not include any unnecessary details.

Ⓑ Writing Skill 2: Acknowledging and Refuting Opposing Solutions
page 165

 4.2 page 166

Possible answers:

1 Although some doctors believe the only way to stop cyberchondria is to tell their patients never to research symptoms online, this is not a realistic plan because it is too convenient for people to look things up online.

2 It may be true that some caregivers prefer face-to-face support groups; nevertheless, it is more convenient for many people to find support online.

3 It is true that cyberbullying can be stopped by having parents prevent their children from bullying, but this will not help when the bully's parents are not available or able to help.

4 While some people argue that doctors save time by connecting to patients on social media, some doctors find that it takes more time and does not reduce patient anxiety.

C Grammar for Writing: It Constructions   page 167

 4.4 page 167

Possible answers:

3 It is inappropriate for doctors to use social media to reach out to patients.
4 It appears that too much time on the Internet can cause health problems like headaches and eye strain.
5 It is likely that many people look up medical information before they go to the doctor.
6 It seems that people who are addicted to the Internet need psychological treatment.

Avoiding Common Mistakes   page 168

 4.5 page 168

The high number of unreliable health websites
is a significant problem, and it is ~~import~~ important to use
only reliable websites when searching the Internet
for health-related information. This simple
solution will solve this problem for many people.
One thing consumers can do is find out who
owns or manages a health website, because
this information can help users decide if a site
is reliable. For example, ~~is~~ it is possible to provide
marketing information on a drug company's
website that seems like it is posted by doctors and
designed for education, when, in fact, the site was
created only to make money for the company.
Some people think it is ~~impossible find~~ impossible to find out who
is behind a website and determine its reliability,
but it is actually very easy. At the bottom of most
sites, users will see a Terms of Use link or a privacy
policy. These legal statements usually list a contact
person or parent company. It is also ~~import~~ important to read
any "About" sections that describe the company,
website, or its goals. This information can help
users decide if the source of the information
is reliable. The most useful websites for health
information are considered reliable because
they are posted by medical organizations and
written by those with medical knowledge. It is
~~impossible find~~ impossible to find out everything about a website or
its content, but smart health consumers need to
understand what they are reading and why it was
published. ~~Is~~ It is one key way to solve the growing
problem of users finding and relying on inaccurate
health information online. Therefore, ~~is~~ it is necessary
to educate consumers of online health information
to use the steps outlined here to research not just
health questions but who is providing the answers
and why.

D Avoiding Plagiarism   page 169

 4.6 page 170

Answers will vary.

6 SUMMARY-RESPONSE ESSAYS

COMMUNICATIONS: THE INFORMATION AGE

page 177

1 *Possible answers:* having to look through multiple sources in order to write a research paper, having too many emails in your inbox, getting more magazines in the mail than you are able to read
2 *Possible answers:* All of your friends have Facebook or similar accounts, but it is hard to see everything they post; you follow so many Twitter accounts that you cannot read them all.
3 In 1996, the World Wide Web had only existed for about two years and was not widely used. This means that Shah experienced information overload from television media, radio, newspapers, magazines, and books.

1 PREPARE YOUR IDEAS

B Reflect on the Topic   page 178

 1.1 page 178

Possible answers:

1 Who curates for readers? Why can't readers curate content for themselves?
2 Why does curation have to offer ways that are creative? Some wine shop employees are probably creative curators.

3 That gives a lot of power to curators to decide what people will know and learn about.

4 I'm actually surprised that the number of photos uploaded each day to Facebook isn't a lot higher than 50 million!

2 EXPAND YOUR KNOWLEDGE

Ⓐ Academic Vocabulary page 180

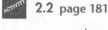 **2.1** page 180

A

| 1 b | 2 a | 3 d | 4 c |

B

| 1 c | 2 d | 3 b | 4 a |

Ⓑ Academic Phrases page 181

2.2 page 181

1 a   2 b   3 b

Ⓒ Writing in the Real World page 182

Possible answers:

"Information overload" occurs when a person is exposed to more information than the brain can process at one time.

Some effects of access to too much information include indecisiveness, bad decisions, and stress.

2.3 page 183

1 Information overload makes you feel overwhelmed by too many choices. Your brain "mildly freezes" and you become paralyzed.

2 Because you can't tell the difference between vital facts and trivial facts.

3 *Answers will vary.*

2.4 page 183

1 The ideas of others.

2 Tartakovsky only included ones that are related to the main idea of her article.

3 Tartakovsky agrees with Palladino that information overload is a problem and has used technology to implement some of Palladino's suggestions. She seems to agree with Burkeman that it is bad to feel you are not in control, but adds suggestions for using technology to regain a feeling of control.

3 STUDY ACADEMIC WRITING

Ⓐ Student Model page 184

Analyze Writing Skills pages 186–187

1 "Stop Knocking Curation" by Steven Rosenbaum

"In his article 'Stop Knocking Curation,' Steven Rosenbaum argues that…"

2 Some of his points were unclear; the author did not consider the point of view of the reader.

3 b

4 "This example" refers to the example of a wine store that is said to be curated.

5 b

6 a

7 a

8 <u>As the amount of information we come across will only increase in the future, I believe the process of content curation will become even more necessary in the future.</u>

 3.1 page 188

1 His two points are that content curation is misunderstood and that it is critical today.

2 The writer believes that wine can be organized by themes, and that this counts as curation because it is similar to the curation of artworks done in a museum.

3 *Answers will vary.*

 3.2 pages 188–189

I Introduction

Source text main idea: In his article "Stop Knocking Curation," Steven Rosenbaum argues that content curation is misunderstood and misused, and asserts that *correct* curation is invaluable for helping us process information on the Internet.

Student's thesis: While I agree with some of his points to an extent, I feel that they could have been clearer, and included the point of view of the reader who is the user of content curation.

II Rosenbaum makes two points

  A Label misunderstood and misused by stores

    1 <u>Stores are collecting – not curating</u>

    2 Definition of true content curation

  B <u>Curation is critical today</u>

    1 So much content on the Internet

    2 <u>Readers need help sorting through it</u>

    3 New roles for journalists

III Disagree with author's examples
  A Wine store example of misuse – unconvincing
    1 Museum curators – paintings on theme
    2 <u>Curators of wine stores are like museum curators</u>
    3 Author should have given more explanation
IV Agree that curators necessary – to an extent
  A Facts and figures are compelling
    1 No time to read or look through data
    2 <u>curation could be "filtering"</u>
  B Curation is job of journalists – questionable
    1 Readers must think for themselves
    2 <u>Content curation is everyone's job</u>
V Conclusion

B Summary-Response Essays
page 190

 3.3 page 190

1 1
2 2
3 3 and 4
4 5

 ·3.4 page 191

Possible answer:
In her article "Overcoming Information Overload," author Margarita Tartakovsky explains that information overload can cause the brain to work too hard and make people feel stressed, but can be controlled.

 3.5 page 192

a 2   b 5   c 4   d 1   e 3

 3.6 page 193

Possible answers:
1 Steven Rosenbaum writes in his article "Stop Knocking Curation" that content curation is very necessary in today's world.
2 In support of this idea, the author states that over 50 million photos are posted to Facebook every day, along with nearly a million hours of YouTube videos and hundreds of billions of emails.

3.8 pages 194–195

1 B   2 B   3 B   4 B

 3.9 page 195

Paragraph B does a better job of using the strategies.

 3.10 page 196

a 3   b 2   c 4   d 1

4 SHARPEN YOUR SKILLS

A Writing Skill 1: Language for Summarizing page 198

 4.1 page 198

1 In the article "Overcoming Information Overload,"
2 According to Margarita Tartakovsky,
3 The author states that
4 As Tartakovsky points out in her article,
5 In the article "Overcoming Information Overload,"
6 The author further states that

B Writing Skill 2: Neutral and Unbiased Language page 199

 4.3 page 200

1 Professors at this university generally <u>dislike/have an issue with</u> [not *hate*] Wikipedia and say that students must never use it, but I think that is a <u>problematic</u> [not *ridiculous*] policy.
2 The <u>chair</u> [not *chairman*] of the new company is <u>illogical</u> [not *crazy*].
3 <u>Police officers</u> [not *policemen*] in Chicago arrested a student for illegal downloading. They seem to think this will stop illegal downloading throughout the city, which is <u>naïve/ill-considered</u> [not *stupid*].

C Writing Skill 3: Avoid Overuse of Key Words page 201

 4.4 page 202

Possible answers:
1 Tim Berners-Lee's creation of the World Wide Web is regarded as one of the most important innovations of the twentieth century. <u>His innovation</u> has changed the way most people in the world get their information.

2 Indries Shah felt that people today have access to too much information, and that <u>they</u> are in danger of drowning in <u>it</u>.

3 There is an enormous amount of information on the web right now. The amount of time required to read all of <u>it</u> exceeds the time any of us have. Also, the supply of <u>data</u> exceeds the demand.

4 The invention of Transmission Control Protocol (TCP) allowed the movement of data on the Internet. <u>This development</u> was the result of research by Vint Cerf and Bob Kahn.

⒟ Grammar for Writing: Noun Clauses page 202

 4.5 page 203

1 what you want to find out
2 how they felt about going online
3 what fits on the counter
4 how long you scan for information
5 what information I need to find; how I am going to find it
6 how you decide to approach information overload

Avoiding Common Mistakes page 203

 4.6 page 204

Paul Baker's article brought up many ideas about social media sites that I had not considered before. Whether or not a person can be addicted to these sites ~~are~~ *is* is something that I have wondered myself. What ~~does the author say~~ *the author says* about Facebook is especially relevant to me. I often find myself checking Facebook several times per hour. The article is very persuasive about the dangers of overusing social media. It has forced me to consider ~~why do I need~~ *why I need* to check Facebook so often. *What I have noticed* ~~What have I noticed~~ is that I often see comments and photos which describe and show my friends doing fun things. Very often, these plans and activities look more fun than what I am doing. This causes me to wonder if knowing about other people's activities makes me dissatisfied with my life. It's not actually necessary for me to know

what everyone is doing ~~what is everyone doing~~ all the time. In addition, what I see on Facebook about other people's lives *gives* ~~give~~ an inaccurate picture. My friends' days are usually probably just as ordinary and unremarkable as my own. Baker says, "Sometimes, it's as simple as taking a 'Facebreak.'" That's a good suggestion, well stated. I do think I need to reduce the amount of time I spend looking at Facebook and comparing my life to the lives of others. The article has therefore provided me with some valuable advice.

⒠ Avoiding Plagiarism page 205

 4.7 page 206

- Authors did survey. 8,353 people

- 8 of 10 respondents had a hard time starting their research project. **paraphrase**

- They had a hard time "determining the nature and scope of what was expected of them." **quote**

- Half of students → not sure how to finish or evaluate their research. **paraphrase** "Nagging uncertainty." **quote**

- "Frustrating open-endedness." **quote** Both for classes and in private lives. **paraphrase**

- My opinion: I agree with the survey. I am insecure about assignments too.

⑦ ARGUMENTATIVE ESSAYS

SOCIOLOGY: SOCIAL INTERACTION

page 213
1 *Answers will vary.*
2 *Answers will vary.*

1 PREPARE YOUR IDEAS

⒝ Reflect on the Topic page 214

1.1 page 214

Possible answers:

Yes/Positve: girls participate in class more when boys aren't there; girls will be more encouraged to take classes in math and science; girls-only classes are easier than coed classes for teachers to manage

No/Negative: boys and girls can learn from each other; without girls, boys-only classes would be too difficult to manage

2 EXPAND YOUR KNOWLEDGE

Ⓐ Academic Vocabulary page 216

2.1 page 216

A

1 d	2 a	3 b	4 c

B

1 c	2 d	3 b	4 a

Ⓑ Academic Collocations page 217

2.2 page 217

1 a	2 b	3 b	4 a	5 b

Ⓒ Writing in the Real World page 218

Answers will vary.

2.3 page 219

1 Dunbar's Number is the maximum number of real friends that a person can maintain. According to Dunbar this number is 150.
2 The central problem is whether social media "friends" are actually real friends in the traditional sense of the word.
3 *Answers will vary.*

2.4 page 219

1 Evidence:
All of paragraph 6
Paragraph 7: "In 2009, *The Economist* found that the average number of Facebook friends per user was 120."
2 "Personally, I think… All of this brings me to the conclusion that the term 'friend' on social media is not a very useful or appropriate one. Perhaps the term 'followers' as used on Twitter or 'connections' as used on LinkedIn are more accurate than Facebook's 'friends' when it comes to defining our social media relationships."

3 STUDY ACADEMIC WRITING

Ⓐ Student Model page 220

1 The writer must give an opinion about whether girls and boys should learn in separate classrooms.
2 *Possible answers:* **In support:** Girls learn better and gain more confidence in girls-only classrooms. **Against:** Girls-only classrooms do not prepare girls for the real world.

Analyze Writing Skills pages 220–222

1 a "In contrast to coed classes, single-sex education means that only students of one gender will be in a class together. In some countries, all schools are single-sex. In other countries, such as the United States, students can choose a single-sex school only if there is one close by. The number of single-sex schools is rising in the United States, but educators disagree on the benefits of them."

b "In my opinion, girls should learn in girls-only classes because they become more self-confident and perform better in math and science." The writer will take the side that girls should learn in girls-only classes.

2 a, c
3 b
4 *Answers will vary.*
5 b
Paragraph 4 is different because it gives reasons why some people disagree with the writer's point of view.
6 "Girls-only classes must be available everywhere to make that possible."

3.1 page 222

1 The advantages of girls-only classes are that girls experience greater success in school and they gain increased confidence and performance in math and science classes.
2 The writer believes that girls don't do well in coed math and science because they do not get support. Girls tend to have more positive attitudes toward math and science in single-sex classrooms.
3 *Answers will vary.*

3.2 pages 222–224

I Introduction
Thesis statement: Girls should learn in girls-only classes because girls become more self-confident and perform better in math and science.

II More confidence
  A Personal experience at a girls-only high school
    1 <u>Less shy</u>
      a Free to express ourselves and take risks
      b <u>Participated more</u>
  B <u>HERI report</u>
    1 Compared freshman girls from mixed sex and girls-only schools
      a Difference in confidence, public speaking skills, computer skills
III Do better in math and science and more positive attitudes
  A Shapka and Keating study
    1 Compared effects of girls-only and coed classes in math and science
      a Grades were 5 percent higher
  B HERI report
    1 <u>Math and verbal skills – 40 points higher</u>
    2 More likely to plan for careers in technology and engineering
IV <u>Critics – single-sex classes reinforce stereotypes</u>
  A Emphasizes differences
    1 Girls – more passive, boys – more aggressive
  B <u>Park, Behrman, and Choi – does not reinforce stereotypes</u>
    1 Girls in single-sex and coed physics classes
    2 <u>physics – not only for boys</u>
V Conclusion

B Argumentative Essay with Refutation page 224

 3.3 page 225

a 4   b 2   c 5   d 1   e 3

 3.4 page 226

Possible answers:

1 Unlike coed classes, in single-sex classes the students are either all male or all female. Boys-only classes are common in many countries around the world, although they are less common in the United States.

2 Supporters of boys-only schools believe that this way of education can help boys build character and follow the rules. Opponents think that it is better for boys to be used to being in coed environments when they are young so that they can get along with women as adults.

 3.6 pages 227–228

1 W; just a statement of fact
2 S; it contains the topic, the writer's opinion, and the main reasons for it
3 W; it doesn't contain the writer's opinion
4 S; it contains the topic, the writer's opinion, and the main reasons for it
5 W; only introduces the topic in the first person

 3.7 page 228

Possible answer: 3. Teaching children at home is an excellent way to make sure that a child learns in a safe environment and learns ideas that are important to the family.

 3.8 page 230

1 b
2 a "All major companies today use various types of social media to improve their customer base, such as Facebook, Twitter, and Instagram."
  b "5.6 percent more revenue"
  d "A recent study found … customers who never participate."

 3.9 page 231

Body paragraph 1: b, d
Body paragraph 2: a, c

 3.10 page 231

1 a S; supports the opinion
  b W; isn't directly related to the opinion
2 a W; doesn't show how businesses lose money
  b S
3 a W; doesn't show how it hurts the business
  b S

 3.12 page 233

Possible answers:

2 Some critics say that coed classes prepare children better for the real world. They learn how to interact appropriately with members of the opposite sex, which they will need to do in the workplace when they are adults.

3 Some opponents state that online friends are not "real" friends. Many online friends are people you have never met or only know slightly.

4 Critics may argue that schools have a responsibility to stop cyberbullying. Cyberbullying often starts with face-to-face bullying in the school.

5 Some people claim that competition is healthy in the workplace. It allows different ideas to be heard, with the best idea winning.

 3.13 pages 234–235

Possible answers:

2 Although it is true that some teens abuse this responsibility, the majority of them want to be trusted and will use their phones responsibly to earn that trust.

3 I agree that online communication is important in the workplace. However, it is simply not true that the only important thing to know for the workplace is how to use email. Many other skills are important, and some of them are not easily taught online.

4 That may be so, but if a person is applying for a job with a high public profile, such as CEO, they should not expect as much privacy, and the company has a right to know what can be seen about the applicant online.

 3.14 page 235

Restated thesis: "In conclusion, social media companies may have different policies, but that does not mean that they cannot have one in common."

Recommendation/call to action: "…all social media sites must agree to a shared policy that requires users to use real names and validate identities when registering."

Arguments: (1) "Requiring people to use real names online makes children safer on social media…" (2) "…prevents scammers from taking advantage of people." (3) It also allows people to find old friends and connections easily…"

4 SHARPEN YOUR SKILLS

Ⓐ Writing Skill 1: Audience and Appeal page 236

 4.1 page 237

1 take action
2 very little
3 expert
4 values
5 open

Ⓑ Writing Skill 2: Language for Introducing Counterarguments and Refutation page 238

 4.3 page 239

1 in favor of
2 argument
3 This may be so
4 According to
5 critics

Ⓒ Grammar for Writing: Complex Noun Phrases page 240

 4.4 page 240

1 Companies worry about employees wasting time on Facebook.

2 Cell phone abuse is a concern for parents with teenagers.

3 Today there are many popular websites used for social networking. / Today there are many popular websites that are used for social networking.

4 The researchers compared girls in single-sex and coed classes.

5 The report looked at boys who were competing against girls.

6 The students were taking online classes offered/ being offered by private universities. / The students were taking online classes that were offered/being offered by private universities.

Avoiding Common Mistakes page 241

 4.5 page 241

One reason cell phones make people worse at maintaining relationships is because of texting. First, ~~people prefer~~ *people who prefer* to text instead of call will try to have whole conversations with someone in very short messages, which can cause confusion. Short texts cannot communicate what voices and conversations can. ~~People talked~~ *People talking* on the phone can hear pauses and changes in tone, which results in clearer communication. For example, for a parent ~~which~~ *who* wants to know if her child is safe, a phone call is very important. Beyond this, texting teaches and reinforces poor writing skills, which can affect ~~those looked~~ *those looking* for jobs. For example,

~~high schoolers text~~ *high schoolers who text* often use abbreviations and spell words incorrectly. This problem has recently been identified by U.S. universities. Many students ~~which~~ *who* need better grammar skills now must take courses to improve their writing so they can make a good impression on future employers. Texting is just one way that cell phones have a negative effect on ~~people want~~ *people who want* to maintain relationships and social skills.

Avoiding Plagiarism page 242

 4.6 page 243

Three things to avoid plagiarism:

1 Title: Fig. 1 Positive technology experiences in relationships
2 Source: Amanda Lenhart and Maeve Duggan, "Couples, the Internet, and Social Media: The Main Report." *Pew Research Center.* Pew Research Center, 11 Feb. 2014. Web. 9 Aug. 2014.
3 Reference in text: As figure 1 shows, the longer a couple is together, the less they use the Internet and cell phone in their relationship. If only the information in the chart were included in the paper, you would need an in-text citation and a citation in Works Cited.

8 TEST TAKING

TIMED WRITING

page 249

1 *Possible answer:* Being organized is an important skill because you spend less time searching for things when you need them. You know where everything is.
2 *Answers will vary.*
3 *Answers will vary.*

1 CHALLENGES OF TIMED WRITING

page 250

 1.1 page 250

Answers will vary.

2 ANALYZE THE WRITING PROMPT

page 251

 2.1 page 252

1 a   2 c   3 b   4 e   5 d

 2.2 page 252

1 *Possible answer:* 1. The topic is the preservation of historic buildings. Key words are "historic buildings," "preserved," and "torn down." 2. The question is asking whether historic buildings should be preserved even if the buildings require a lot of money to maintain. 3. There is one part to the question. 4. The essay is an argumentative essay because of the words "agree" and "disagree."
2 *Possible answer:* 1. The topic is growing up in the city versus in a small town. Key words are "growing up," "city," and "small town." 2. The question is asking how growing up or being raised in a city and a small town are different. 3. There is one part to the question. 4. The essay is a comparison and contrast essay because of the word "differ."

 2.3 page 253

1 *Possible answer:* 1. The topic is "learning from mistakes." 2. The question is asking you to choose a mistake, describe it, and tell what was learned and how life changed. 3. There are two parts. 4. The essay is mainly a cause and effect essay because of the words "learned from" and "impact," but it will include narrative because of the word "describe."
2 *Possible answer:* 1. The topic is "how different generations communicate." 2. The question is asking you to compare how someone born before 1970 and someone born after 1995 communicate differently. 3. There are two parts. 4. The essay is mainly a comparison and contrast because of the word "different", but it also includes cause and effect because of the word "change."

3 PLAN YOUR WRITING

page 254

 3.1 page 256

Possible answers:

1 I'd make a chart and list how I thought the two were similar in one column and then how they were different in another column.

2 I would use a cluster diagram and list things in circles and then add reasons for each one.

 3.2 page 256

Possible answers:

Prompt 1.

Brainstorm method will vary.

Possible outline:

I Introduction:
   Thesis: Volunteering is necessary for the world.

II Good for society
   – Makes us work together
   – Makes us care
   – Doctors Without Borders organization

III Makes children become less selfish
   – Stop thinking about themselves
   – My example

IV Countries – disasters
   – Countries need supplies and help
   – Example – tsunami

V Conclusion

Prompt 2.

Brainstorm method will vary.

Possible outline:

I Introduction:
   Thesis: School is not the major part of a child's education

II Values make us good people
   – Values must be taught at home
   – School can't teach

III Reading at home
   – Read and learn by themselves
   – My example

IV Social organizations
   – Religious institutions and communities
   – Museums, concerts, etc.

V Conclusion

4 WRITE YOUR ESSAY

page 257

 4.1 page 258

Answers will vary.

5 PROOFREAD

page 259

 5.1 page 260

Answers will vary.

 5.2 page 260

Answers will vary.

6 APPLY WHAT YOU HAVE LEARNED

page 261

A Student Model page 261

 6.1 page 263

1 She plans her time.
2 She proofreads her essay and makes corrections.
3 She spends one minute.
4 She spends 30 minutes writing her essay.

NAME: ....

DATE: ....

Part A: Academic Vocabulary

Circle the correct words to complete the sentences.

1 Many local businesses have made **a commitment / an alternative / a coincidence** to help their communities.

2 There is **ethical / widespread / exposed** thought that the companies consumers buy from should try to make the world a better place.

3 Some shoppers consider buying from locally owned businesses to be **an ethical / a radical / a widespread** choice because they can see how shopping locally benefits their community.

4 Small farmers' markets offer **widespread / excessive / alternative** choices for shoppers who prefer locally grown produce.

5 Small business owners can offer unique services such as painting or cooking classes that **expose / coincide / commit** shoppers to experiences not available in large chain stores.

6 Many large stores take advantage of Black Friday, the Friday after Thanksgiving, which **alternates / exposes / coincides** with a day that most Americans do not have to go to work – an ideal shopping day.

7 When the first stores began opening at midnight on Thanksgiving for Black Friday shoppers, it seemed like a really **radical / alternative / ethical** idea.

8 Many Black Friday deals are very unfair and lead to **ethical / excessive / committed** purchasing of unnecessary items, which wastes consumers' money.

Part B: Academic Collocations

Complete the sentences with the academic collocations in the box.

an alternative approach	excessive consumption	a widespread belief
coincides with	make a commitment	

1 Increased social media use .... the increased use of smartphones.

2 Smartphone applications for retail chains' discount cards and coupons offer .... to carrying discount cards and coupons.

3 Cell phone providers are asking whole families to .... to them and to their products for two years.

4 Instead of labeling teens' heavy texting as .... , cell phone companies are offering an inexpensive unlimited text message package to the whole family.

5 There is .... among teenagers that their parents do not use their cell phones as much as they do.

SCORE: .... / 16

NAME: ....   DATE: ....

Part A

Complete the sentences with a gerund or infinitive form of the verbs in parentheses.

1 One of the disadvantages of .... (order) online is high shipping costs.

2 Many online retailers tend .... (offer) free shipping if customers spend a minimum amount of money.

3 Some retailers offer "free" gifts with a minimum purchase, encouraging consumers .... (spend) more than they normally would.

4 Advertisers might want .... (think) about whether or not a decrease in live television viewing affects sales.

5 Bad weather can be responsible for .... (delay) the shipment of goods, which disappoints many online consumers.

6 The benefits of .... (send) electronic invitations include saving money on print cards and stamps and helping party planners track responses.

7 Popular online review websites help customers choose .... (eat) in the best-rated restaurants.

8 Consumers can avoid .... (support) bad businesses by consulting consumer websites.

Part B

Complete the sentences with a passive gerund or infinitive form of the verbs in parentheses.

1 The successful entrepreneur agreed .... (interview) by the marketing students.

2 Many customers at expensive shops expect .... (serve) by experienced, knowledgeable staff.

3 One benefit of goods .... (sell) online is that company employees don't need to meet their customers face to face.

4 The older chef needed .... (expose) to new cooking trends to remain successful.

5 Consumers who are interested in .... (offer) discounted prices at the local home goods store must sign up online.

6 The new business owner wanted .... (invite) to join the local business group where she could meet other business owners.

7 The children's bookstore manager enjoyed .... (be / know) as a positive influence in his community.

8 The retail employees proposed .... (pay) overtime for working during holidays.

NAME: ....   DATE: ....

Part A

Match the words with their meanings.

.... 1 plagiarism

.... 2 academic integrity pledge

.... 3 citing sources

.... 4 quotation marks

.... 5 paraphrasing

a the punctuation you place around the original author's exact words in your essay

b restating the original author's ideas in your own words

c copying other people's exact words or ideas without identifying who said or wrote them

d a contract with your school that says you will be honest in your studies

e identifying the places where you got information in your essay

Part B

Circle the correct MLA citation form.

1 Author:

   a Solomon, Richard R.

   b Richard R. Solomon.

2 Magazine article title:

   a *The Future of Shopping Trends.*

   b "The Future of Shopping Trends."

3 Printed book title:

   a *Consumer Behavior: Buying, Having, and Being.*

   b "Consumer Behavior: Buying, Having, and Being."

4 Dates in online information:

   a Sept. 14, 2013. Retrieved Dec. 3, 2014.

   b 14 Sept 2013. Web. 3 Dec. 2014.

5 Online government report:

   a Environmental Protection Agency, United States.

   b United States. Environmental Protection Agency.

Instructors: This is a list of possible prompts to assign as a unit writing quiz.

1 In many street markets, it is common for buyers and sellers to negotiate prices. In retail establishments, however, there is usually a set (or firm) price. Should consumers be able to negotiate prices in retail stores? Why or why not?

2 Many small local stores close because they can't compete with the low prices and convenient shopping of large chain stores. Whose responsibility is it to keep small local stores open – the business owners or the customers? Explain.

3 Bartering – the exchange of one service for another without spending money – has been around for thousands of years. For example, a baker might have exchanged a loaf of bread for a basket of fruit from a farmer. In today's economy, do you think there are benefits to bartering? Explain.

4 These days, more and more people are shopping online. Do you think online shopping will be the only way to shop in the future? Why or why not?

5 Some children and teens try to earn money by offering services to neighbors such as yard work, babysitting, or selling lemonade. Should they be required to purchase a business license or permit? Why or why not?

NAME: ....   DATE: ....

Part A: Academic Vocabulary

Circle the correct words to complete the paragraph.

In 2014, I prepared to move from my home in India to join my aunt, uncle, and cousins in Toronto,

Canada. I was glad to have the **security / complexity / initially** of family and a place to live in

(1)

my new country. At the same time, I **adjusted / anticipated / imaged** that I would have certain

(2)

difficulties once I arrived in Canada related to language, customs, and other issues. When I first arrived,

I was **securely / initially / stressfully** so busy that I didn't find the time to become anxious. Soon,

(3)

however, the experience became quite **stressful / initial / secure** because many aspects of life were

(4)

so new. The **ambitions / complexities / securities** of this new world – understanding Canadian

(5)

English, learning the streets, and finding simple things like grocery stores and dry cleaners – added

to the stress. What helped me was that I always maintained an **ambition / adjustment / image** of

(6)

myself as a Canadian – living and working in this wonderful culture. After a year in Canada, I was

able to realize my **ambition / complexity / adjustment** of assimilating into Canadian society with a

(7)

good job, a nice apartment, and many new friends. I had never realized how difficult it would be to

anticipate / stress / adjust to the Canadian lifestyle, but I am truly glad I did it.

(8)

Part B: Academic Phrases

Complete the paragraph with the academic phrases in the box.

for the sake of	in the case of	over the course of

.... the writer from India in Part A, it took time to adjust to life in Canada.

(1)

She endured the hardships of being an immigrant .... her lifelong dream of becoming

(2)

Canadian. .... a year, she became more used to life in Canada.

(3)

NAME: ....   DATE: ....

Part A

Complete the sentences with the correct past tense form.

1   During the 1840s, Boston .... a large increase of Irish immigrants due to the potato famine in Ireland.
    a   had been experiencing   b   experienced

2   The international student population at the community college .... by the time the ESL department was established.
    a   had doubled   b   was doubling

3   Immigration records .... readily available by the time I began researching my family history last year.
    a   had been becoming   b   had become

4   A large number of immigrants .... through Ellis Island in the early 20th century.
    a   were passing   b   passed

5   Mario became interested in immigrating to Australia while he .... about the country.
    a   was reading   b   read

6   Many foreign residents of Paris .... French before they arrived in the city.
    a   were learning   b   had learned

7   The English professor had been living in Beijing for two years before she .... Mandarin.
    a   had studied   b   studied

8   Some Saudi Arabian companies .... their employees to study English in the U.S. before they could continue working at the company.
    a   required   b   were requiring

Part B

Complete the paragraph with the correct past tense form of the verbs in parentheses.

In the early twentieth century, many young women from Canada moved to Massachusetts to work in the textile mills. One young woman, Emilie Meuse, ... (hear) of opportunities to earn reasonable (1) wages in the mills. Though her family had no desire or need to leave Canada, Emilie was different. Not only did she want to earn money, she also wanted to fulfill her dream of living in the United States. Since she .... (sew) her own clothes since she was a young girl, Emilie .... (know) she could get a (2)   (3) job at a mill easily. By the time she .... (be) ready to leave for the United States, Emilie .... (4)   (5) (become) a young woman of 15. On the boat to Massachusetts, Emilie .... (search) the newspapers (6) for job vacancies when she .... (meet) another girl, Sarah. The two girls .... (become) (7)   (8) good friends, and much to their joy, both .... (find) jobs in the same mill. By the time the (9) girls .... (return) home ten years later, they realized how difficult their life .... (be) in (10)   (11) Massachusetts. With Sarah's encouragement, Emilie .... (write) about this important piece of (12) American history in a memoir.

NAME: ....

DATE: ....

Part A

Check (✓) the information that is common knowledge.

- [ ] 1 Facts common to your major or field
- [ ] 2 Studies or research by other people
- [ ] 3 Common myths, legends, or holidays
- [ ] 4 Scientific theories or philosophical ideas
- [ ] 5 Statistics and data
- [ ] 6 Common scientific or historical facts
- [ ] 7 Original opinions or ideas
- [ ] 8 Common current topics of discussion

Part B

The sentences below are from an essay. Check (✓) the sentences that should be cited.

- [ ] 1 Ellis Island received 12 million immigrants between the years 1892 to 1954.
- [ ] 2 People have been emigrating to other countries throughout history.
- [ ] 3 July 4 marks the day that Americans celebrate their independence from Britain.
- [ ] 4 Many Chinese left China for Taiwan during the early part of the twentieth century.
- [ ] 5 Over 125,000 Cubans arrived in Florida during the Mariel Boatlift of 1980.
- [ ] 6 Dr. Mark O'Neill contends that most Irish left Ireland because of British mistreatment.
- [ ] 7 Genealogy research can help find the paths immigrants took.
- [ ] 8 In 2010, immigrants made up 35 percent of the population of Los Angeles.

Instructors: This is a list of possible prompts to assign as a unit writing quiz.

1 Think of the reasons that you or someone you know immigrated to a new land. Describe the physical and emotional journey.

2 Have you or someone you know ever regretted moving to a new house, town, or country? Tell the story.

3 Tell the story of someone who moved to a place that was culturally very different. How did he or she deal with life in the new culture?

4 Some people are married to spouses from cultures different than their own. Think of someone you know who married someone from another culture and tell his or her story.

5 Tell a story about you or someone you know who moved to a new country temporarily. How did the trip change his or her life after returning home?

SCORE: .... / 13

NAME: ....   DATE: ....

Part A: Academic Vocabulary

Circle the correct words to complete the paragraph.

In China, earning a degree from an American or British institution can **enhance / exhibit / summarize**
(1)

one's employability. Young Chinese people often choose to earn those degrees,

mutually / subsequently / sustainedly returning home to China to have families and care for their
(2)

parents. Parents are willing to have their children spend years studying overseas because it brings

exhibited / subsequent / mutual benefits to both generations: children will have good jobs and parents
(3)

will have better care as they age. The success of these professionals with degrees earned outside of China

sustains / reacts / summarizes the continued trend of students studying overseas. If employers in China
(4)

had a different **document / reaction / exhibit** to applicants with foreign degrees, this trend would
(5)

certainly not continue. Some parents, however, worry that their children will not return to China, as

reacted / sustained / documented in a recent study. A report that **summarized / enhanced / sustained**
(6)   (7)

the results of the study showed that the majority of students do return to China. In addition, these young

professionals **reacted / documented / exhibited** the ability to work in growing international industries such
(8)

as trade and education, which further strengthens their connections to their communities.

Part B: Academic Collocations

Complete the sentences with the correct form of the academic collocations in the box.

exhibit behavior	greatly enhance	mutual benefit	mutual support	negative reaction

1 The trade agreement provided .... to both countries: one received needed raw materials
   and the other received needed manufactured goods.

2 According to a study, business travelers may have a .... to companies that are new to
   them; on the other hand, they are comforted when they find familiar things in unfamiliar places.   .

3 Study participants said they felt that their relationship with these companies was based on
   ...., as if they shared a common goal and wanted to help each other.

4 Satisfied business travelers .... that indicates familiarity and happiness, such as smiling and
   thanking employees.

5 Studies show that increased migration has .... people's understanding of different
   cultures.

SCORE: .... / 14

NAME: ....

DATE: ....

Part A

Complete the sentences with the present perfect or the present perfect progressive form of the verb in parentheses.

1 Once the land of opportunity, California .... (experience) a reverse immigration trend recently: many native Californians are moving to other states for better work and housing opportunities.

2 Social media .... (make) it easier for people to stay connected to loved ones and friends, regardless of where they live.

3 Many young professionals .... (choose) to live in smaller cities as opposed to large cities.

4 Smaller cities .... (attract) younger people with an increased variety of international foods lately.

5 Urban centers .... (offer) international foods as well, perhaps to keep young professionals in big cities.

6 The population of my college town .... (decrease) more this summer than in previous summers.

7 Snowbirds – northerners from the northeastern United States and Canada – .... (escape) the cold northern winters for warm, sunny South Florida for decades.

Part B

Complete the paragraph with the present perfect or the present perfect progressive form of the verb in parentheses.

Hawaiian surfers .... (ride) the gentle waves of Oahu's south shore for centuries. Visitors to the
    (1)
islands quickly discovered the joys of the sport, and since the 1940s people .... (surf) in oceans

all over the world. Due perhaps to its tropical origins, surfing .... (be) seen as a warm water
                                                                    (3)
sport. However, since those early days, wetsuit technology .... (improve). Wetsuits, rubber-like
                                                            (4)
suits that swimmers and surfers wear to keep warm, used to be awkward, uncomfortable, and unreliable.

Recently, they .... (get) lighter, warmer, and more comfortable. These improvements ....
            (5)   (6)
(allow) wave riders to discover new surfing locations in colder places such as Alaska, Scotland, and Norway.

Surfing .... (become) a truly global sport. Surfers now migrate from coast to coast in search of the
        (7)
perfect waves.

NAME: ....

DATE: ....

Part A

Check (✓) the things you should do to write a good paraphrase.

- [ ] 1 Read the material carefully for meaning.
- [ ] 2 Memorize the material.
- [ ] 3 Take notes on all main and supporting ideas.
- [ ] 4 Include the source in your notes.
- [ ] 5 Write the paraphrase from memory, or use your notes to help you.
- [ ] 6 Use the same language as the original author.
- [ ] 7 Use varied sentence structure.

Part B

Read the quotations and paraphrases. There is a problem with each paraphrase. Circle the letter of the problem.

1 **Quotation:** "The Canadian Employment Ministry in June 2014 announced that fast-food, retail and hotel industries could not obtain new low-wage, low-skilled temporary foreign workers if the jobless rate in their region exceeds six percent. Canadian employers can have a maximum of 30 percent temporary foreign workers in 2014, 20 percent in 2015, and 10 percent in 2016."

    Source: Migration News. UC Davis. October 2014, Volume 21, Number 4. Web. 27 March 2015.

    Paraphrase: According to the Canadian Employment Ministry, fast-food, retail, and hotel industries couldn't get low-wage workers in 2014 if the Canadian jobless rate exceeds six percent. During that year, Canada could employ a maximum of 30 percent foreign workers.

    Problem:

    a The writer did not include the source.

    b The writer used the original writer's exact words.

    c The writer changed the meaning of the original writer's words.

2 **Quotation:** "By the late 1990s, the US was taking in about 1m immigrants a year: 730,000 legal immigrants, 200,000 illegal aliens and about 100,000 refugees. About 70% of legal immigrants are admitted for the purposes of family reunification."

    Source: Hall, Ben. "Immigration in the European Union: problem or solution?" OECD Observer ©Prospect Magazine, June 2000 / OECD Observer No 221–222, Summer 2000.

    Paraphrase: Of the approximately one million immigrants to the United States in the late 1990s, most were legal, numbering 730,000. Seventy percent of those came to the U.S. to be reunited with family members. At that same time, refugees to the U.S. numbered roughly 100,000 while 200,000 immigrants were considered illegal.

    Problem:

    a The writer did not include the source.

    b The writer used the original author's exact words.

    c The writer changed the meaning of the original author's words.

(CONTINUED)

3 **Quotation:** "Rapid growth in the black immigrant population is expected to continue. The Census Bureau projects that by 2060, 16.5% of U.S. blacks will be immigrants."

> Source: Anderson, Monica. "A Rising Share of the U.S. Black Population Is Foreign Born." *Pew Research Center*. 9 April 2015. Web. 1 April 2015.

Paraphrase: The Census Bureau says that 16.5% of the U.S. population will be black by 2060 because it's growing so rapidly, according to the Pew Research Center.

Problem:

a The writer did not include the source.

b The writer used the original author's exact words.

c The writer changed the meaning of the original author's words.

Instructors: This is a list of possible prompts to assign as a unit writing quiz.

1 Some cities are home to a lot of new residents who have moved there for work or school. What effects does this new population have on those who are permanent residents?

2 Many young people move from rural communities to cities to get better jobs. How has this affected both cities and rural communities? Are the effects positive, negative, or both? Discuss.

3 "Gentrification" is the purchase and repair of homes in poorer urban areas by those with better finances. How has gentrification affected those who have lived in these areas for generations, the neighborhood, and local businesses?

4 Some parents send their children overseas to study. How does this affect the relationship between these parents and their children?

5 It has become somewhat popular for American retirees to sell their homes and move into retirement communities. What effects does this change have on retirees' lifestyles?

NAME: ....

DATE: ....

Part A: Academic Vocabulary

Circle the correct words to complete the paragraph.

One difference between life 100 years ago and life today is the availability of food. In the past, the

availability of certain fruits was **altered / conditioned / restricted** to the seasons in which they grew.
(1)

For example, consumers in North America could only expect to have peaches in the summer and apples

in the autumn. This situation is different today because advances in technology, such as refrigeration

and transportation, have **concentrated / altered / restricted** the way fruit is stored and sold. Oranges
(2)

can travel thousands of miles and arrive in good **condition / commodity / consequence** in distant
(3)

places. This year-round availability of food has contributed to an increase in the availability of fast food.

To fight against this increase in fast food, Carlo Petrini began the Slow Food movement in Italy in 1986.

The movement emphasizes that food should be from local sources and cooked slowly. Since then, it has

spread to other countries. The Slow Food movement is **conditioned / concentrated / altered** mostly in
(4)

developed countries. Supporters of this movement dislike how **virtually / conditionally / dramatically**
(5)

people's attitudes toward food have changed in the past century. They feel that people should be more

aware of where their food comes from and value their local food traditions. They also feel strongly that a

consequence / restriction / concentration of certain aspects of the modern food industry is that our planet
(6)

is being **conditionally / alternatively / virtually** destroyed. Supporters of the Slow Food movement do not
(7)

see food simply as **an alteration / a commodity / a consequence**, but as a feature of life that should be
(8)

enjoyed slowly with others.

Part B: Academic Phrases

Complete the paragraph with the academic phrases in the box.

are likely to	in the same way	it is important to note

Nutritionists say that when we think about what to eat, ... that fresh fruit and
(1)

vegetables play an essential role in healthy eating. Fruits .... be sold in the same form
(2)

that they were on a tree, bush, or vine – in other words, in their natural state. ....,
(3)

fresh vegetables that are sold in their natural state are preferable to canned vegetables that may include

harmful additives such as salt. Nutritionists emphasize we should eat plenty of fresh fruits and vegetables to

avoid illness and weight gain.

NAME: ....   DATE: ....

Part A

Identify the noun or noun phrase and its appositive phrase in each sentence. Circle the noun and underline its appositive phrase.

1 Indian food, a typically spicy cuisine, can be ordered with little or no spice in the United States.

2 Tourists in the Bahamas like to order peas and rice, a staple food of the island country.

3 Saffron, a favorite local Thai restaurant, offers both vegetarian and gluten-free dishes.

4 A traditional Spanish dish, paella, is made with rice, chicken, shellfish, and vegetables.

5 Escargot, the French word for "snail," is delicious despite its unappetizing look and texture.

6 It is easy to order Chinese food without MSG – monosodium glutamate – nowadays.

7 A necessary element for bone health, calcium, can now be found in food and drinks such as orange juice as well as in dairy foods.

Part B

Correct the mistake in the appositive in each sentence.

1 Food trucks, which trucks equipped to cook and serve food, are becoming a popular dining option for food enthusiasts.

2 Both amateur and professional chefs can be seen in food competition shows TV programs in which people compete to make the best food in front of judges.

3 San Diego has a lot of farm-to-table restaurants, are restaurants that source and serve food from local farms.

4 Trout a kind of freshwater fish is a common menu item in the Blue Ridge Mountain region of North Carolina.

5 Shopping at a farmers' market, street market featuring local produce, meat, and homemade baked goods, is a great way to support local food producers.

6 The U.S. FDA – which the United States Food and Drug Administration – requires that all food sold in supermarkets list ingredients and nutritional information.

NAME: ....

DATE: ....

Part A

Check (✓) the credible sources for use in a research paper about sustainable farming.

☐ 1 a friend who writes novels about farming life

☐ 2 a professor of agriculture at your university

☐ 3 a gossip magazine about celebrities who now farm

☐ 4 a scholarly journal on recent large-scale farm practices in the midwestern U.S.

☐ 5 a BBC website article on small farm protests in the UK

Part B

Check (✓) the three best sources for a research paper about the organic food movement.

☐ 1 an article about organic food in the Massachusetts Institute of Technology (MIT) Press magazine published in 2011

☐ 2 a Wikipedia entry on the organic food movement

☐ 3 a *Washington Post* article on a study of organic crops and pesticides, written in 2014

☐ 4 a daily blog about eating an organic diet

☐ 5 a *New York Times* article comparing supermarkets and health food stores, published in 1979

☐ 6 an article about the safety of organic ingredients from the U.S. Food and Drug Administration's website

Instructors: This is a list of possible prompts to assign as a unit writing quiz.

1 The proverb "Eat to live; don't live to eat" means that eating should be something you should do to maintain health, not a fun activity. Compare and contrast people who live to eat and people who eat to live.

2 Think of two distinct regions in your country. Compare and contrast the food culture in both regions.

3 Do men and women eat differently? Compare and contrast them.

4 Compare and contrast fresh and frozen fruits and vegetables.

5 Compare and contrast the advantages and disadvantages of making home-cooked foods and eating fast food.

NAME: ....

DATE: ....

Part A: Academic Vocabulary

Circle the correct words to complete the sentences.

1 Doctors need to be able to communicate quickly with patients who experience **anxiety / probability / tendencies** between appointments.

2 There is an **irrational / apparent / anxious** connection between patients' stress levels and wait time for doctors to provide them with test results.

3 The patients' appointments, phone calls, and stress are all **probable / demonstrated / triggered** by new symptoms or increased pain.

4 Patients' fears can seem **irrational / logical / probable** because there may not be a good reason to think they need immediate medical attention.

5 From the patient's point of view, the **logical / triggered / demonstrated** thing to do might be to contact the doctor and make sure everything is fine.

6 Since many patients have a **probability / tendency / trigger** to worry about medical issues, doctors have begun to use social media such as blogging to help patients outside of office hours.

7 Some doctors send mass email notifications of new blog posts to reduce the **probability / anxiety / logic** that patients will seek time-consuming answers to general questions.

8 To help patients with anxiety, some doctors provide **triggers / logic / demonstrations** of the anxiety-reducing techniques described in their posts and messages.

Part B: Academic Collocations

Complete the paragraph with the correct forms of the academic phrases in the box.

basic logic   clearly demonstrate   high probability   irrational tendency   logical conclusion

There are several ways that parents can help children who are victims of cyberbullying. While

.... would say that staying connected to bullies online is unhealthy, children might
(1)

not realize this without their parents' help. They can also monitor their children's Internet use and try to stop

their .... to stay connected to bullies on social media. While some parents can help
(2)

their children, research .... that many teenagers need outside help, perhaps from a
(3)

school counselor or psychologist. Without this help, there is a .... that cyberbullying
(4)

will continue. The .... is that the problem of cyberbullying needs to be prevented
(5)

because it is doing so much harm to these young people.

NAME: ....

DATE: ....

Part A

Complete the sentences with the correct it construction.

1 .... at reviews of doctors on the Internet before contacting one.

   a It is common to look   b It is common for look   c It common to look

2 Some doctors say .... with them after certain medical procedures.

   a it is necessary check   b it necessary that check   c it is necessary to check

3 .... a second opinion before undergoing surgery.

   a It is recommend you to get   b It is recommended that you get   c Is recommended you get

4 .... your medical history online through your doctor's office's website.

   a Is easy to check   b It is easy you check   c It is easy to check

5 Nowadays, during patient visits .... a patient's notes by hand; many doctors type notes directly into a patient's electronic medical file.

   a it seem unusual to record   b it seems unusual record   c it seems unusual to record

6 .... strangers' unreliable stories of their medical problems on some websites.

   a It is not advisable to believe   b It is not advisable for believe   c Is not advisable believe

Part B

Correct the mistake in each sentence.

1 It is important for people use reliable websites to research cures for medical problems.

2 It might harmful for children to have smartphones.

3 Instead of asking family or friends, it is better seeking medical advice from doctors.

4 Is necessary for high schools to offer classes to students about the dangers of cyberbullying.

5 It might be better people to use different email addresses for their work and personal correspondence.

6 When visiting places with high occurrences of infectious diseases, is crucial to check government websites for health warnings.

7 Instead of consulting a doctor, it seems for many people are more likely to read about illnesses on the Internet.

8 It appears that children to have more access to the Internet nowadays than ever before.

NAME: ....

DATE: ....

Part A

Check (✓) the good time management strategies when writing an essay.

- [ ] 1 Make a list of tasks you need to do.
- [ ] 2 Write down a start and finish date or time for each task.
- [ ] 3 Don't worry about revising if you are a good writer.
- [ ] 4 Wait until the day before it is due to start writing.
- [ ] 5 Plan how much time to spend on each task in advance.
- [ ] 6 Get help from an instructor, classmate, or friend if needed.
- [ ] 7 Spend as much time as possible conducting Internet research.

Part B

Read each scenario. Circle the letter of the time management strategy each student should use.

1 Carlos has to write a problem-solution essay about students texting in class. He feels overwhelmed because he has so much to organize before he even starts writing. What should he do?

   a Divide the project into a list of smaller tasks.

   b Cross off each task when it is completed to see progress.

   c Leave time at the end to review and revise the essay.

2 Marcia tends to spend too much time on the Internet researching her topic. Then she doesn't have enough time to write her essay. What should she do?

   a Avoid procrastination.

   b Look at the due date and decide when she needs to start.

   c Decide how much time is needed to spend on each task.

3 Frank has written the first draft of his essay, but he hasn't had a chance to rewrite it before tomorrow's due date. What should he do?

   a Look at the due date and decide when you need to start.

   b Leave time at the end to review and revise the essay.

   c Divide the project into a list of smaller tasks.

4 Justin made a list of things to do for his essay. Since he has been really busy with his other classes and work, he isn't sure which tasks he has completed. What should he do?

   a Leave time at the end to review and revise the essay.

   b Look at the due date and decide when he needs to start.

   c Cross off each task when it is completed to see progress.

Instructors: This is a list of possible prompts to assign as a unit writing quiz.

1 Some people are addicted to social media and feel they have to constantly let others know everything that is going on in their lives. What are some of the problems this might cause on both a personal level and to society as a whole?

2 How can middle-aged businesspeople with limited knowledge of social media gain needed skills to use it in their businesses?

3 Today high school clubs often communicate with members through social media alone. However, some younger high school students are not allowed to have social media accounts. What are some problems with requiring these students to join social media sites?

4 What can schools do to make students use electronic devices such as smartphones and tablets for educational purposes only while in school?

5 Some people go to online discussion boards and forums for information about prescription medicine. What problems can using these sites cause?

NAME: ....   DATE: ....

Part A: Academic Vocabulary

Circle the correct words to complete the paragraph.

The main idea of Andrew Baum's article "Obtaining and Using Information on the Job" is that there are negative aspects of information overload that we need to understand. Baum contends that when we receive increasingly larger amounts of information, it is **constant / inevitable / minimized** that we will experience a
(1)
decrease in concentration and focus. Baum points to studies showing that if the amount of information that needs to be processed **exceeds / attributes / deviates** someone's processing abilities, his or her ability to
(2)
think clearly can be **established / inevitable / minimized** or even reduced to zero. He concludes that people
(3)
should **attribute / establish / dismiss** a list of clear questions that need to be answered before searching for
(4)
information, and that these be used as a guide throughout the research process. I agree with Baum's article, and I think too many workers **dismiss / deviate / exceed** the dangers of information overload. Most people
(5)
in the workplace understand very well that the Internet can be a waste of time. Most of them have dealt with the **deviate / constant / minimal** temptation to play a game or message a friend rather than work.
(6)
In addition, many students have sometimes **dismissed / established / attributed** an inability to complete
(7)
their homework to distractions on their computers. I agree with one of Baum's points quite strongly: workers and students should establish a practice of making a list of clear questions that need to be answered before conducting research. I think if they follow this practice and try not to **dismiss / attribute / deviate** from it,
(8)
they can ignore distractions and get their work done.

Part B: Academic Phrases

Complete the paragraph with the academic phrases in the box.

at the same time	part of the	the idea of

Zhang really makes it clear how .... collaboration was key to the two
(1)
computer scientists' early achievements. He points out that while they worked closely together over the years, ..., Bosworth and Sanchez did not always agree on things.
(2)
.... reason that this article is so well written is that Zhang is able to take complex ideas
(3)
about technology and explain them to a non-expert reader in a clear way.

NAME: ....   DATE: ....

Part A

Circle the correct words to complete the sentences.

1 I'm not sure **how / where** bloggers can think of so many topics to write about on a daily basis.

2 Students conducting research on the Internet must determine **whether / which** a source is trustworthy or not.

3 Employers have the right to give a warning to employees **how / when** they spend time on social media sites during work hours.

4 **If / Which** political advertisements appear on a website, most readers who have a different viewpoint will seek other sources for news.

5 With so many options of communication available today, it is hard to decide **whether / which** method is best.

6 Nowadays, no matter **when / where** people live, they can stay connected to the rest of the world easily.

Part B

Correct the mistake in each sentence.

1 I will stop reading those newspapers which they continue to charge fees for online access to articles.

2 Whether or not people are smarter today with access to a large amount of information on the Internet, it is debatable.

3 Whether or not students post to classroom discussion boards are still an option in my classes.

4 It helps me stay on top of my assignments when does my professor use our class website to post homework.

5 How students can determine which ideas to annotate in a text are a skill they will learn in this class.

6 News websites that offers unbiased news stories are generally more reliable.

SCORE: .... / 6

NAME: ....

DATE: ....

Part A

Match the students' scenarios with the letter of the best note-taking strategy.

<u>Scenario</u>

.... 1 For her essay on Steve Jobs, Rosaria did Internet research using her notebook computer in a coffee shop. She doesn't type well, so she takes notes on paper. She forgot her notebook, so she wrote her notes on coffee napkins.

.... 2 Thomas read a lot of interesting data from experts in the information technology field for his essay. He took a lot of notes, but now he forgets if he copied the ideas from the texts or if he changed the language.

.... 3 Simon took ten pages of notes on his topic of expanding access to technology to Third World countries. He needs to incorporate this information in his paper, but he doesn't remember where he got all of the information.

<u>Note-Taking Strategy</u>

a Write all the source information at the top: authors, titles, dates, mediums, and pages.

b Take notes in a notebook, on index cards, or in a document on the computer.

c Use big quotation marks and write the word *quote* for exact words, and write *paraphrase* when you restate someone's words.

Part B

Read the excerpt from an original source and Jonah's notes. Check (✓) the problems with his notes.

Text from Original Source

"Teens are increasingly sharing personal information on social media sites, a trend that is likely driven by the evolution of the platforms teens use as well as changing norms around sharing. A typical teen's MySpace profile from 2006 was quite different in form and function from the 2006 version of Facebook as well as the Facebook profiles that have become a hallmark of teenage life today. For the five different types of personal information that we measured in both 2006 and 2012, each is significantly more likely to be shared by teen social media users on the profile they use most often.

- 91% post a **photo of themselves**, up from 79% in 2006.
- 71% post their **school name**, up from 49%.
- 71% post the **city or town where they live**, up from 61%.
- 53% post their **email address**, up from 29%.
- 20% post their **cell phone number**, up from 2%.

"Generally speaking, older teen social media users (ages 14–17), are more likely to share certain types of information on the profile they use most often when compared with younger teens (ages 12–13)."

Source: Madden, Mary, et al. "Teens, Social Media, and Privacy." Pew Research Center. 21 May 2013. Web. 13 April 2015.
http://www.pewinternet.org/2013/05/21/teens-social-media-and-privacy/

(CONTINUED)

Jonah's Notes

- Teens share personal info on social media changes in sharing norms
- MySpace and Facebook profiles different in 2006 than in '12
- 5 different types surveyed in '06 and '12:
  QUOTE:
  "91% post a **photo of themselves**, up from 79% in 2006.
  71% post their **school name**, up from 49%.
  71% post the **city or town where they live**, up from 61%.
  53% post their **email address**, up from 29%.
  20% post their **cell phone number**, up from 2%"

- Older teens share on the profile most used – more than younger kids

☐ 1 no source listed

☐ 2 content of original text changed

☐ 3 no quotations around quoted material

☐ 4 missing information at top of note page: date, page number, author, medium

☐ 5 no indication of paraphrased material

Instructors: This is a copy of "Stop knocking curation (adapted)" from page 184 of the Student's Book (without the annotations). The students have already read it in class. You can assign it as a unit writing quiz with the following directions:

1 Read the article again and annotate it.

2 Write a summary and response. Use your own ideas.

Curation is the act of finding and organizing information on a topic online, while also providing links to the original content. Companies that benefit from using content curation include the Huffington Post, an insightful online news aggregator and blog, and Reddit, a popular website where contributions from its community members provide for amusing discussions and tales from the world of entertainment, news, and social networking.

Stop knocking curation Steven Rosenbaum (adapted)

Curation is a growing concept as the enormous volume of mostly identical content has made it nearly impossible for mere mortals to find useful, thoughtful, contextual content on the Web. But its practice is undervalued. In just one example, a 2012 writing in *The Atlantic* called "curate" one of the "words we'd just as soon never write or see or hear spoken again."

I disagree. Information overload **inevitably** drives content consumers to look for human-filtered, journalist-vetted, intellectually related material. This demand for coherence isn't unreasonable; it's essential. And for those who think and write every day, gathering bits of ideas here and there that can be turned into a thoughtful narrative "on a topic" isn't cheating, or being lazy. Far from it. For those who would **dismiss** or **minimize** curating, it is in many ways harder than writing (at least *good* curating is). It's far easier for me to write 500 words from my head than to find themes and sources and tie them into a broader narrative.

Now, my issue with the current state of curation is that there are many people who wrongly attribute misguided meanings to the word. In so doing, they **deviate** from the core concepts that make curation so appealing and relevant.

Curation started as a term for a practice that was emerging over the past few years to filter the overabundance of data and create quality, thoughtful, human-organized collections. The most urgent need for curation was in Web content. This is because there is far too much data being produced by digital devices, video-enabled mobile phones, auto-tweeting devices, and overzealous Facebook friends. Curators create entirely new editorial works by finding, filtering, and contextualizing. Meaning is produced from within massive amounts of data.

(CONTINUED)

Curation, in its purest form, helps to **establish** a solution to a problem that meets a growing need. But then a bunch of random marketers and sign makers got in the act. Today, things are curated that shouldn't be. For example, a wine store can be known as a "social wine store" (whatever that means) if it claims to provide "curated" craft beer and spirits. As if another wine shop isn't "curated" (heck, they just stock whatever boxed wine they can get their hands on).

If the word *curation* is allowed to be diluted to simply mean "selected" or "quality collection," then it no longer solves the problem we need it to solve. Content *needs* curation. The **constant** overflow of unfiltered content would overwhelm us if there was no one to objectively organize and watch over it. Wine doesn't pose this problem.

Here are a few scary stats: Everyday, 50 million photos are uploaded to Facebook, 864,000 hours of video are uploaded to YouTube, and 294 BILLION emails are sent. That's why you can't read all the mail you get anymore.

This all makes curation an important, even essential, part of journalism. The world is full of meaningless data. Readers are hungry for clarity and understanding. And journalists are trained to find meaning and assemble facts into something that can be rationally and logically understood. They're rewarded with enlightened readers, engaged audiences, and a revitalized role in the new world. In this new world, anyone can be a creator of information. Quality curation is a wonderful thing.

Adapted from "Stop Knocking Curation" by Steven Rosenbaum, www.cjr.org/the_kicker/leave_curation_alone.php.
Reproduced with permission of Columbia Journalism Review.

SCORE: .... / 13

NAME: ....   DATE: ....

Part A: Academic Vocabulary

Circle the correct words to complete the paragraph.

It is important for young people to have complete freedom in choosing their friends. The main

reason is they need to be able to make their own **constraints / conclusions / evidence** about who
(1)

is a good friend and who is not. **Perception / Capacity / Evidence** from various studies shows that it
(2)

is healthy for children to make their own choices in friendships, as long as parents are aware of these

friendships. Young people are more honest with each other without adults around, which means that

children have a better **conclusion / constraint / perception** of who their peers are than any adult.
(3)

Parents may **equate / select / constrain** their children's choices in friends to an inability of becoming
(4)

successfully independent. However, children have the **evidence / stability / capacity** to choose friends
(5)

that may lead to long-lasting and **stable / selective / constraining** friendships. They are naturally
(6)

capable / stable / selective about the friendships they make. Parents choosing friends for their children is
(7)

an unfair **conclusion / constraint / selection** on young people who must learn, grow, and make mistakes
(8)

in relationships. If young people cannot make these mistakes, they cannot learn how to choose friends.

Part B: Academic Collocations

Complete the paragraph with the academic phrases in the box.

draw conclusions	popular perception	strong evidence
have the capacity	stable relationship	

There is a .... among many parents that children should learn how to
(1)

communicate online from a very young age. However, this is not necessarily true. While younger children

may .... to use a computer or smartphone, it does not mean that they are old
(2)

enough to understand the online world. Parents need to protect their children until they can understand

and .... about the content they are reading. Until there is ....
(3)   (4)

showing that it is safe for young children to communicate online, it is better not to allow them to do so until

they are older. If parents can establish a .... with their children by offering support
(5)

and modeling good Internet behavior, it is the first step in educating kids about how to use the Internet

responsibly.

NAME: .... DATE: ....

Part A

Circle the correct words to complete the sentences.

1 Single-gender classes **at / which / what** some schools use different activities to teach the same concepts to both boys and girls.

2 Teachers **who / which / for** teach in single-gender schools may receive special training on the ways boys and girls learn differently.

3 Boys **what / who / from** prefer hands-on activities enjoy spatial and experiential learning.

4 Girls typically like to participate in verbal activities **which / in / who** class, including discussions and debates.

5 Some studies show that older boys and girls **who / which / about** are in single-gender classrooms are more comfortable because there is less pressure.

6 Single-gender classes **which / what / in** lower grades offer more chances for gender-specific play.

7 Schools that offer single-gender education appeal to some parents **who / at / what** want their children to focus more on academic study.

Part B

Correct the mistake in reduced relative clauses in each sentence below.

1 Many people live in Miami, Florida come from all over Latin America, the Caribbean, and the northern United States.

2 It is impossible to go anywhere in Miami without hearing a variety of languages included English, Spanish, Creole, and Portuguese.

3 Those looked for better living conditions moved to the cities in the last half of the twentieth century.

4 There is a lot of delicious Latin American food waits in every part of Miami.

5 Lively social customs represent the many different cultures can be found all over the city.

6 People move to this city today have the opportunity to learn about and understand different cultures.

NAME: ....

DATE: ....

Part A

Circle the correct words to complete the sentences.

If you include a graph or chart in your essay:

1 Set the graph or chart close to the **text / source / Work Cited page** that refers to it.

2 Include the word **summary / reference / figure** and its number, and a short caption above the graph or chart.

3 Include **a summary / information / a citation** about the source below the graph or chart.

4 Refer to the figure in your essay and write a **reference / text / summary** of the information in the graph or chart.

5 Do not include a **citation / figure / text** in Works Cited if you write the source below the chart or graph.

6 If you refer to a graph or chart, but do not include it in your essay: Include an in-text **summary / reference / information** like all other citations, and include a citation in Works Cited.

Part B

A student wants to use this graph in an essay. What needs to be added to avoid plagiarism? Label the graph with the phrases from the box. You will not use all of the phrases.

a graph label	a short explanation of the information in the graph	today's date
recent statistics	the source	

1 ....

Internet has Most Positive Influence on Education, Least Positive on Morality

Meridian saying increasing use of internet has had a ..... on...

Good influence   Bad influence   No influence

Education	64%	18%	8%
Personal relationships	53	25	10
Economy	52	19	15
Politics	36	30	16
Morality	28	42	12

2 ....

3 ....

* Asked in 32 emerging and developing developing nations.

Source: Spring 2014 Global Attitudes surver. Q75a–e.

PEW RESEARCH CENTER

Instructors: This is a list of possible prompts to assign as a unit writing quiz.

1 Do you agree or disagree with some companies' policy of checking applicants' credit history in addition to professional and personal references?

2 Do you think that mental health is as important as physical health? Should society support both equally? Why or why not?

3 Some people believe that birth order determines people's personalities: first-born children are achievers and controlling; middle children are peacemakers and popular; last-born children like attention and are out-going; and only children (children without siblings) are more adult and good leaders. Do you agree or disagree that birth order makes a difference in personality? Explain.

4 In his poem *Mending Wall,* the American poet Robert Frost wrote, "Good fences make good neighbors." This means that it is easier to get along with your neighbor if you both respect each other's privacy. Do you agree or disagree with this idea? Explain.

5 Politics, religion, and money are three topics Americans generally avoid during social gatherings. Do you think that these topics should be avoided at social gatherings? Why or why not?

6 Today, many primary and secondary schools in the United States – both public and private – require school uniforms. Some believe it allows students to focus on learning, while others think it prevents students from expressing themselves as individuals. Do you think schools should require uniforms? Explain.

UNIT QUIZZES ANSWER KEY

UNIT 1

Unit 1 Vocabulary
Part A
1 a commitment	5 expose
2 widespread	6 coincides
3 an ethical	7 radical
4 alternative	8 excessive

Part B
1 coincides with	4 excessive
2 an alternative	consumption
approach	5 a widespread belief
3 make a commitment	

Unit 1 Grammar
Part A
1 ordering	5 delaying
2 to offer	6 sending
3 to spend	7 to eat
4 to think	8 supporting

Part B
1 to be interviewed	5 being offered
2 to be served	6 to be invited
3 being sold	7 being known
4 to be exposed	8 being paid

Unit 1 Avoiding Plagiarism
Part A
1 c   2 d   3 e   4 a   5 b

Part B
1 a   2 b   3 a   4 b   5 b

UNIT 2

Unit 2 Vocabulary
Part A
1 security	5 complexities
2 anticipated	6 image
3 initially	7 ambition
4 stressful	8 adjust

Part B
1 In the case of	3 Over the course of
2 for the sake of	

Unit 2 Grammar
Part A
1 b	3 b	5 a	7 b
2 a	4 b	6 b	8 a

Part B
1 had heard	7 met
2 had been sewing	8 became
3 knew	9 found
4 was	10 returned
5 had become	11 had been
6 was searching	12 wrote

Unit 2 Avoiding Plagiarism
Part A
Check: 1, 3, 6, 8

Part B
Check: 1, 5, 6, 8

UNIT 3

Unit 3 Vocabulary
Part A
1 enhance	5 reaction
2 subsequently	6 documented
3 mutual	7 summarized
4 sustains	8 exhibited

Part B
1 mutual benefits	4 exhibit behavior
2 negative reaction	5 greatly enhanced
3 mutual support	

Unit 3 Grammar
Part A
1 has been	4 have been attracting
experiencing	5 have been offering
2 has made	6 has decreased
3 have chosen	7 have been escaping

Part B
1 have been riding	5 have gotten
2 have been surfing	6 have allowed
3 has been	7 has become
4 has improved	

Unit 3 Avoiding Plagiarism
Part A
Check: 1, 4, 5, 7

Part B

1 b   2 a   3 c

UNIT 4

Unit 4 Vocabulary

Part A

1 restricted   5 dramatically
2 altered   6 consequence
3 condition   7 virtually
4 concentrated   8 a commodity

Part B

1 it is important to   2 are likely to
note   3 In the same way

Unit 4 Grammar

Part A

1 Noun: Indian food
Appositive Phrase: a typically spicy cuisine
2 N: peas and rice
AP: a staple food of the island country
3 N: Saffron
AP: a favorite local Thai restaurant
4 N: paella
AP: A traditional Spanish dish
5 N: Escargot
AP: the French word for "snail"
6 N: MSG
AP: monosodium glutamate
7 N: calcium
AP: A necessary element for bone health

Part B

1 Food trucks, ~~which~~ trucks equipped to cook
and serve food, are becoming a popular dining
option for food enthusiasts.

2 Both amateur and professional chefs alike
can be seen in food competition shows, TV
programs in which people compete to ᵛmake
the best food in front of judges.

3 San Diego has a lot of farm-to-table restaurants,
~~are~~ restaurants that source and serve food from
local farms.

4 Trout, a kind of freshwater fish, is a common
    ᵛ   ᵛ
menu item in the Blue Ridge Mountain region
of North Carolina.

5 Shopping at a farmers' market, ᵃstreet market
                                   ᵛ
featuring local produce, meat, and homemade
baked goods, is a great way to support local
food producers.

6 The U.S. FDA – ~~which~~ the United States Food
and Drug Administration – requires that all
food sold in supermarkets list ingredients and
nutritional information.

Unit 4 Avoiding Plagiarism

Part A
Check: 2, 4, 5

Part B
Check: 1, 3, 6

UNIT 5

Unit 5 Vocabulary

Part A

1 anxiety   5 logical
2 apparent   6 tendency
3 triggered   7 probability
4 irrational   8 demonstrations

Part B

1 basic logic   4 high probability
2 irrational tendency   5 logical conclusion
3 clearly demonstrates

Unit 5 Grammar

Part A

1 a   2 c   3 b   4 c   5 c   6 a

Part B

1 It is important for people ᵗᵒuse reliable websites
                              ᵛ
to research cures for medical problems.
2 It might ᵇᵉharmful for children to have
            ᵛ
smartphones.
3 Instead of asking family or friends, it is better
to seek
~~seeking~~ medical advice from doctors.
It is
4 ~~Is~~ necessary for high schools to offer classes to
students about the dangers of cyberbullying.
                              for
5 It might be better ᵖeople to use different
                      ᵛ
email addresses for their work and personal
correspondence.

6 When visiting places with high occurrences of infectious diseases, *it* is crucial to check government websites for health warnings.

7 Instead of consulting a doctor, it seems ~~for~~ *that* many people are more likely to read about illnesses on the Internet.

8 It appears that children ~~to~~ have more access to the Internet nowadays than ever before.

Unit 5 Avoiding Plagiarism

Part A
Check: 1, 2, 5, 6

Part B
1 a   2 c   3 b   4 c

UNIT 6

Unit 6 Vocabulary

Part A
1 inevitable   5 dismiss
2 exceeds   6 constant
3 minimized   7 attributed
4 establish   8 deviate

Part B
1 the idea of   3 Part of the
2 at the same time

Unit 6 Grammar

Part A
1 how   4 If
2 whether   5 which
3 when   6 where

Part B
1 I will stop reading those newspapers ~~which~~ *if* they continue to charge fees for online access to articles.

2 Whether or not people are smarter today with access to a large amount of information on the Internet~~, it~~ is debatable.

3 Whether or not students post to classroom discussion boards ~~are~~ *is* still an option in my classes.

---

4 It helps me stay on top of my assignments when ~~does~~ my professor ~~use~~ *uses* our class website to post homework.

5 How students can determine which ideas to annotate in a text ~~are~~ *is* a skill they will learn in this class.

6 News websites that ~~offers~~ *offer* unbiased news stories are generally more reliable.

Unit 6 Avoiding Plagiarism

Part A
1 b   2 c   3 a

Part B
Check: 1, 4, 5

UNIT 7

Unit 7 Vocabulary

Part A
1 conclusions   5 capacity
2 Evidence   6 stable
3 perception   7 selective
4 equate   8 constraint

Part B
1 popular perception   4 strong evidence
2 have the capacity   5 stable relationship
3 draw conclusions

Unit 7 Grammar

Part A
1 at   3 who   5 who   7 who
2 who   4 in   6 in

Part B
1 Many people ~~live~~ *living* in Miami, Florida come from all over Latin America, the Caribbean, and the northern United States.

2 It is impossible to go anywhere in Miami
  without hearing a variety of languages ~~included~~ *including*
  English, Spanish, Creole, and Portuguese.
3 Those ~~looked~~ *looking* for better living conditions moved
  to the cities in the last half of the twentieth
  century.
4 There is a lot of delicious Latin American food
  ~~waits~~ *waiting* in every part of Miami.
5 Lively social customs ~~represent~~ *representing* the many
  different cultures can be found all over the city.
6 People ~~move~~ *moving* to this city today have the
  opportunity to learn about and understand
  different cultures.

Unit 7 Avoiding Plagiarism

Part A
1 text   4 summary
2 figure   5 citation
3 information   6 reference

Part B
1 a graph label
2 a short explanation of the information
  in the graph
3 the source

UNIT QUIZZES WRITING RUBRIC

Final Draft Writing Assignment Rubric

CATEGORY	CRITERIA	SCORE
Language Use	Grammar and vocabulary are accurate, appropriate, and varied. Sentence types are varied and used appropriately. Level of formality (register) shows a good understanding of audience and purpose. Mechanics (capitalization, punctuation, indentation, and spelling) are strong.	
Organization & Mode (structure)	Writing is well-organized and follows the conventions of academic writing: • Paragraph – topic sentence, supporting details, concluding sentence • Essay – introduction with thesis, body paragraphs, conclusion Rhetorical mode is used correctly and appropriately. Research is clearly and correctly integrated into student writing (if applicable).	
Coherence, Clarity, & Unity	Sentences within a paragraph flow logically with appropriate transitions; paragraphs within an essay flow logically with appropriate transitions. Sentences and ideas are clear and make sense to the reader. All sentences in a paragraph relate to the topic sentence; all paragraphs in an essay relate to the thesis.	
Content & Development (meaning)	Writing completes the task and fully answers the prompt. Content is meaningful and interesting. Main points and ideas are fully developed with good support and logic.	

How well does the response meet the criteria?	Recommended Score
At least 90%	25
At least 80%	20
At least 70%	15
At least 60%	10
At least 50%	5
Less than 50%	0
Total Score Possible per Section	25
Total Score Possible	100

Feedback: